Comments on THE MEDICINE WHEEL

"The time is right for THE MEDICINE WHEEL to be received. Our culture's precarious condition—psychological, social, ecological—requires healing and stabilizing. Earth astrology will certainly help many to do that. I have the deepest trust in Sun Bear's vision; I have equally deep trust in the medicine ways he and Wabun offer us to restore healthy relations among people and the Earth."   —John W. White

"Out of a secure traditional wisdom that once maintained the harmony of Creation in this land, Sun Bear and Wabun bring a needed message to the children of a confused and disintegrating civilization. It is a message of balance, of self-reliance, of attunement with the spirits of the natural world—skills well nigh lost to our overspecialized, pre-packaged, left-brained education. This is more than just another system of personality classification and analysis. It is a compendium of fascinating information about various animals, minerals and plants, including their characteristics, their healing and spiritual qualities, as well as the uses made of them by the native people of this continent. This is a new vision, a vision for our times."   —Medicine Story

THE MEDICINE WHEEL

Earth Astrology
by Sun Bear and Wabun

Illustrated by Nimimosha and Thunderbird Woman

Prentice-Hall, Inc., Englewood Cliffs, New Jersey

Book Designer. Linda Huber
Art Director, Hal Siegel

The Medicine Wheel: Earth Astrology
by Sun Bear and Wabun

Printed in the United States of America
Prentice-Hall International, Inc., London
Prentice-Hall of Australia, Pty. Ltd., Sydney
Prentice-Hall of Canada, Ltd., Toronto
Prentice-Hall of India Private Ltd., New Delhi
Prentice-Hall of Japan, Inc., Tokyo
Prentice-Hall of Southeast Asia Pte. Ltd., Singapore
Whitehall Books Limited, Wellington, New Zealand

10 9 8 7 6 5 4 3 2 1

Library of Congress Cataloging in Publication Data

Sun Bear (Chippewa Indian)
The medicine wheel.
1. Indians of North America—Religion and mythology.
2. Astrology. I. Wabun, joint author. II. Title.
E98.R3S93   299'.7   79-26146
ISBN 0-13-572982-3

TO
NIMIMOSHA, WABOOSE,
SPARROW HAWK, YARROE,
SHAWNODESE, NOKOMIS,
THUNDERBIRD WOMAN, and MOONFLOWER
and those others who have and will share
our lives and vision

and to the Spirits of the
ancient builders of the Medicine Wheels
who shared their vision with us

⛏ Contents

Acknowledgments

We wish to thank all of the many people, over the years, who have shared their lives and hearts with us. Through this sharing, we have been able to see enough of our fellow two-leggeds to write about them. We have at least two hundred people come to share with us at our home each year, so it is impossible to acknowledge them all by name but they know who they are. There are some who have been with us throughout the actual writing of this book, and they deserve special thanks for their love, patience and support. They are Nimimosha, Waboose, Yarroe, Sparrow Hawk, Thunderbird Woman, Gloria Acosta, Lynne van Mansen, and Misha. Others who were here giving love, support and special help on the book are Robyn Klein, who corrected and typed the final manuscript, Tom Huber, who shared his knowledge of metaphysical subjects in correcting and commenting upon both the original and the final manuscripts, and Ramona Owen, who did reading that cut down a lot on our research time. Thanks also to Bernard and Robert James.

We also wish to thank all of our relations in the mineral, plant and animal kingdoms who share this land and their energy with us. Special thanks to our dogs, Shasta and Tsacha, who are always there with encouragement and energy.

We wish to thank our editor, Oscar Collier, a friend who helped us to see what this book could give to people.

For correspondence or conversation on the history and uses of the Medicine Wheel by different tribes we wish to thank Lee Piper, Richard Rainbow, Adolf Hungry Wolf, John White, Brad Steiger, Twylah Nitsch, Ruth Hill, Medicine Story, Joan Halifax, Tom and Alice Kehoe, John Eddy, John Carlson, Nakwisi, Pierre, Dorothea Blom and R. G. Forbis. For information on Native uses of plants we thank Norma Myers, director of the Green Shores Herbal School in British Columbia.

A special thanks for the beautiful artwork to Thunderbird Woman and to Nimimosha.

As always our thanks to the Great Spirit for allowing us to be instruments of His will, and to the beautiful Earth Mother who sustains us all.

Author's Note

The foundation of the religion and the life of the Native people in the United States, as well as in most countries if you follow history back far enough, is personal vision, personal communication between the individual and the Creator Spirit, by whatever name this force was called.

Vision can come to individuals in a number of ways. They can go out upon the mountains or into the valleys and cry for their vision. Sometimes it will take many such quests before vision comes, if it ever does. Some visions are whole and complete and give the person receiving it total understanding of the universe and his or her place in it. Other visions come in parts, none of which is complete in itself. Eventually, with patience, enough parts come to make the vision complete.

Visions can also come to people complete in their dreams, and these can be the type that give total understanding. For others, vision might come during an illness, through an experience of dying and returning to life or even in the course of their everyday lives.

When vision forms the foundation of life, the sacred teachers know enough of this experience to help others if help is necessary in interpreting a vision. All people know that they have to give respect to each other's visions at all times. Today, so many people have forgotten that vision is possible that they tend to try to make it a museum relic of the past, an interesting display with no relevance to contemporary life.

We are all born with the capacity to dream and to have vision. This is what makes us humans, the animals who can have vision and seek to fulfill it on the earth plane. This is what makes us reflections of the force that created us all.

This book came about as the result of a vision that I had long ago. In this vision I saw that the time drew near when, for the sake of the Earth Mother and all of our evolution as human beings, we must return to a better and truer understanding of the earth and all of our relations on her. I saw that we would have to put aside the petty fears that divided us and learn to live as true brothers and sisters in a loving way. I saw that we would have to find others who shared our heart's direction, whatever their racial background, and join with them into groups that always remembered that our purpose was to be instruments of the Great Spirit's will and helpers to our Earth Mother. I saw that such groups could greatly effect the cleansing of the earth that is now occurring.

That was the part of my major vision that I can share at this time. Since the time that I had it I have been striving to fulfill it, with good results. I am the medicine chief of the Bear Tribe, a multiracial medicine society based upon that vision, and we reach many people with the work that we do and with the message that we have been entrusted to carry.

Our message can be summed up in the phrase "Walk in Balance on the Earth Mother." This reflects all the attitudes of my people, a people who felt that their lives had to blend with all the things around and within them. They felt, as we do, that we have to come to a point where we truly feel the oneness, the unity, that connects us to all of the universe, and that we have to reflect that unity in all aspects of our lives.

The Medicine Wheel came to me in a more recent vision, one described in this book. After receiving the vision, which showed me how the Medicine Wheel was to be used to teach people, Wabun, who is my medicine helper and wife, worked with me in developing and writing about these teachings. Her knowledge for this came to her through the small visions I have already described.

When we were asked to write a book about this vision of the Medicine Wheel, we felt that such a book could help many others to understand the visions that I have had. We felt that this book could help people to open their hearts to all of their relations on our common Earth Mother. The information in this book came to us through the Great Spirit, through our observation of our relations in the human, animal, plant and mineral kingdoms and through some reading of the observations of others. We have not read or studied astrology, although we have sometimes talked to others who have. The information in this book does not, to the best of our knowledge, conform to any way of gaining self-knowledge used by any particular tribe in the United States. This is a new way revealed to us at this time to help with the healing of the Earth Mother. We attribute any similarities between the Medicine Wheel and astrology or any other way of self-knowledge to the fact that all truths come from the same Source.

That is how this book came to be. Let us open our hearts and share this vision of today. We all share the same Earth Mother, regardless of race or country of origin, so let us learn the ways of love, peace and harmony, and seek the good paths in life. It is good to have spoken.

SUN BEAR

A Vision of the Medicine Wheel

I saw a hilltop bare of trees, and there was a soft breeze blowing. The prairie grass was moving gently. Then I saw a circle of rocks that came out like the spokes of a wheel. Inside was another circle of rocks, nearer to the center of the wheel. I knew that here was the sacred circle, the sacred hoop of my people. Inside of the center circle was the buffalo skull, and coming up through ravines, from the four directions, were what looked like animals. As they came closer, I saw that they were people wearing headdresses and animal costumes. They moved to the circle and each group entered it sunwise, making a complete circle before they settled on their place in the wheel.

First, people came to the place of the North, to the winter, the time of resting for ourselves and the Earth Mother, the place that represents the time when we have the white hairs of snow upon our heads, when we prepare to change both worlds and forms. Then there were those who ended up on the East, the place of awakening, of birth and of spring, the place representing mankind's birth and beginning. Next came those who would represent the South, the time of summer, the years of fruitfulness and of rapid growth. Then there were people who came to the West, the time of fall, when we reap our harvest, when we have found the knowledge needed to center ourselves. The West is the home of the West Wind, Father of All of the Winds.

All the people were singing the song of their season, of their minerals, of their plants, of their totem animals. And they were singing songs for the healing of the Earth Mother. A leader among them was saying, "Let the medicine of the sacred circle prevail. Let many people across the land come to the circle and make prayers for the healing of the Earth Mother. Let the circles of the Medicine Wheel come back."

In this vision were gathered people of all the clans, of all the directions, of all the totems, and in their hearts they carried peace. That was the vision I saw.

 # Medicine Wheel

	DATES	MOON	ANIMAL	PLANT
NORTH	Dec. 22–Jan. 19	Earth Renewal	Snow Goose	Birch Tree
	Jan. 20–Feb. 18	Rest & Cleansing	Otter	Quaking Aspen
	Feb. 19–March 20	Big Winds	Cougar	Plantain
EAST	March 21–April 19	Budding Trees	Red Hawk	Dandelion
	April 20–May 20	Frogs Return	Beaver	Blue Camas
	May 21–June 20	Cornplanting	Deer	Yarrow
SOUTH	June 21–July 22	Strong Sun	Flicker	Wild Rose
	July 23–Aug. 22	Ripe Berries	Sturgeon	Raspberry
	Aug. 23–Sept. 22	Harvest	Brown Bear	Violet
WEST	Sept. 23–Oct. 23	Ducks Fly	Raven	Mullein
	Oct. 24–Nov. 21	Freeze Up	Snake	Thistle
	Nov. 22–Dec. 21	Long Snows	Elk	Black Spruce

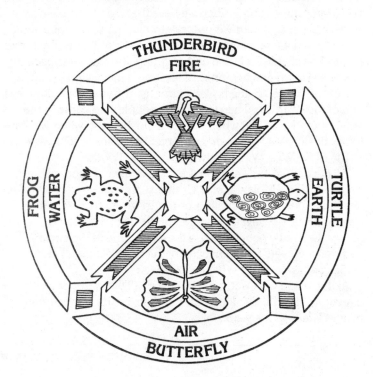

Reference Chart

MINERAL	SPIRIT KEEPER	COLOR	COMPLEMENT	
Quartz	Waboose	White	Flicker	
Silver	Waboose	Silver	Sturgeon	
Turquoise	Waboose	Blue–Green	Brown Bear	
Fire Opal	Wabun	Yellow	Raven	
Chrysocolla	Wabun	Blue	Snake	
Moss Agate	Wabun	White & Green	Elk	
Carnelian Agate	Shawnodese	Pink	Snow Goose	
Garnet & Iron	Shawnodese	Red	Otter	
Amethyst	Shawnodese	Purple	Cougar	
Jasper	Mudjekeewis	Brown	Red Hawk	
Copper & Malachite	Mudjekeewis	Orange	Beaver	
Obsidian	Mudjekeewis	Black	Deer	

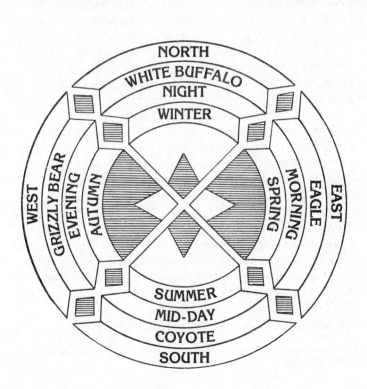

Introduction

T This book is written to reach out and help all people relate better to the Earth Mother and to all the rest of the creation around us. It is designed to help us understand that relationship. Many times we may feel that there is something missing in life. We may feel a longing sense to be closer to nature and the elemental forces. We hope that this book will help you to find your place on the Medicine Wheel, to identify with powers that may have been lost to you. We hope that in finding a kinship with the universe you may understand why this relationship was so cherished by Native people. When you are able to completely blend with all things, then you are truly part of the whole.

The knowledge of the Medicine Wheel is needed at this time. We feel that if humanity is to grow, then we must all come to a closer understanding of our environment. It is man's alienation from natural things that causes many of his ills. Today, many people are trying to restore their balance with nature. People are turning to natural foods and natural healing, and there is a great back-to-the-land movement. Even in our industrialized society we feel the need to restore the balance with nature. It is at this time that we offer you the teachings of the Medicine Wheel.

We invite you, in reading this book, to cast aside your preconceptions and enter, with us, a magical world where all things are connected to you, and you are connected to all things. This magical world consists of the very real and beautiful earth that is always around you and all your relations on her.

We invite you to open your eyes, your ears, your minds and your hearts and to see the magic that is always there. Today we tend to see the earth as a stable backdrop for all of the affairs of humankind. We see the minerals, the plants and the animals as servants of man. We have forgotten that they can be our teachers as well; that they can open us to ideas and emotions that have been blocked from the human heart for too long a time.

We have forgotten that we are connected to all of our relations on the earth, not just our human family. We have forgotten that we have responsibilities to all these relations, just as we have them to our human families. We have imprisoned ourselves in tight little worlds of man-made creations.

We have forgotten how to hear the stories and songs that the winds can bring to us. We have forgotten to listen to the wisdom of the rocks that have been here since the beginning of time. We have forgotten how the water refreshes and renews us.

We have lost the ability to listen to the plants as they tell us which ones of them we should eat to live well. We have lost the ability to listen to the animals as they give us their gifts of learning, laughter, love and food. We have cut ourselves off from all of these relations, and then we wonder how we can so often be bored and lonely.

The Medicine Wheel is a magic circle that encompasses all of that world. As you journey around it, you will find wonders both within and without. With tenacity you will even discover the wonder of knowing about yourself: who you are, what you know and what you can do in this lifetime.

The Native people knew about this magic circle. They respected it and used it often in their everyday lives so they would always remember all of the things that they had learned. When they built their homes, most often these were circles, whether they were tipis, wigwams or hogans. When they went to purify their bodies and their minds, they did so in the circle of the sweat bath, a cleansing lodge which represented the womb of the human mother from whom they came, and the womb of the Earth Mother, who sustained them throughout their lives. When they came together in council, they sat in a circle, so that everyone was included, as an equal, with an equal voice.

When they made music, they made it upon a round drum. They danced in a circle. The beat of the drum represented the beat of their hearts and the beat of the Earth Mother. They raised their arms and legs toward the heavens, and then placed them upon the earth, creating a circle that extended from the earth to the sky and back to the earth, with their bodies as the transmitters.

They saw life as a circle, from birth to death to rebirth. They knew how to acknowledge and celebrate the circles of their own lives so that they were able to flow and change with the changing energies that came with different ages. They knew that they, like the seasons, passed through several phases as the circle of life and time passed around them. They knew that to fall out of this circle was to fall out of rhythm with life and to cease to grow.

The circle was so important to them, so essential to life continuing in the ways that it should, that they immortalized this figure in their ceremonies and structures. The mounds of the mound-building culture were round. The calendars of the Aztecs were round, and the medicine wheels of stone were round. In everything they reminded themselves that the earth and everything on her were part of the magic circle of life.

To remind yourself now of this circle, remember that you are always traveling around it. You enter the circle at one point, and the entrance gives you certain powers, gifts and responsibilities. Your starting point is determined by the moon or month under which you were born. Different starting points are governed by different elemental clans which tell you the element to which you are attached. This clan has nothing to do with the clans of kinship that existed in most tribes. Those were determined by the clans of one's parents, and they, in turn, could govern the earthbound responsibilites one would have, as well as those one could marry. The elemental clans determine your relationship to the elements solely, and, like all of the other points on the Medicine Wheel, these are not static. The starting points are also governed by the Spirit Keeper of their direction.

It was essential for people in the old days to live their lives in such a way that they would continuously be journeying around the wheel. This is equally essential now. To stay with only one moon, one totem, one element, is to become static. To become static is to cease to grow, to cease to know that one has a connection with all of the wheel. It is tantamount to stopping the flow of the life force through your being.

As you pass around the wheel, you have the responsibility of learning about the different moons, totems, plants and elements through which you pass. By this learning you keep your own life in constant change, you keep the life force beating within your heart.

This is the vision that we have of the Medicine Wheel. In this vision we see that it is a way to teach people to change, to grow, to be open to life, to be open to all of their relations on the earth. We see, too, that this vision is a vision for today, when we have forgotten so much that the people used to know. It is a vision that can help people to leave their sometimes lonely and boring existences without having to move anything but their minds and hearts. And for those who are never lonely and bored, it is a way to find even more excitement and companionship in their lives. Most of all, the Medicine Wheel is a way for you to get to know yourself, in all of your many aspects and manifestations.

In our vision, people are not limited by their starting position, direction or clan. They will not always have the strengths and weaknesses of just this one position. *They have to journey as far as they can around the wheel, experiencing the lessons, challenges, strengths and weaknesses of as many of the positions as possible. Every position has something to give them, some gift that will enlarge and enrich their lives.*

The essence of the Medicine Wheel is movement and change. Through this knowledge, people attempt to allow themselves as much room for change in any one life as they can handle. They wish to progress around the wheel and experience as many manifestations of human nature as possible. They know that they contain all of these manifestations within themselves, but they have to place themselves in various positions and experiences in order to feel them. They do not use their starting position as an excuse for behavior that is not as strong and clear as it could be. Rather, when experiencing such behavior, they will try to move themselves to another position where they can feel the strength necessary to wash away the weakness. Sometimes this strength will come from feeling human emotions or thinking human thoughts. Other times it will come from observing an animal, as it goes about its life, and seeing what strengths are within that animal. Or it can come from observing a rock, a plant, or listening to the song of the winds or the heartbeat of the earth.

For those who live in a way that is open to all of the lessons the creation has to teach, the proper lesson will always come at the right time, no matter who the necessary teacher is. For those who live in this way, the earth is a magical place and a source of constant marvels.

We can all live in this way if we choose to allow ourselves to do so. It is only the arrogance of our minds that tells us we are alone in an alien and hostile universe. It is only the pride of our intelligence that tells us we are the most important part of that universe. It is only our fear that makes us feel unloved and alone.

If we open our hearts, the light of the love and unity that created the universe can shine in and illuminate the flat and arid landscape in which we sometimes choose to live. If we start traveling the magic circle, our hearts will naturally begin to open wider as we learn to experience this life we have been given in all of its beautiful aspects.

THE MOONS
AND THE TOTEMS

The moon, or month, during which you were born determines your starting place on the Medicine Wheel and your beginning totem in the mineral, plant and animal kingdoms. The first moon of the year, the Earth Renewal Moon, marks the time when the Father Sun returns from his journey to the south and begins, once again, to precipitate growth in the Earth Mother and all of her children. This moon begins at the time of the winter solstice, which usually occurs on December 22. This is the first moon of Waboose, Spirit Keeper of the North. It is followed by the Rest and Cleansing Moon and the Big Winds Moon. The moons of Waboose, those of rest and renewal, bring the time to contemplate the growth of the previous year and prepare for the growth of the year to come.

Following the moons of Waboose are those of Wabun, Spirit Keeper of the East. These three moons are those of awakening growth, when the Father Sun begins to illuminate all of earth's children and prepare them to bring forth their proper fruit. The first moon of Wabun is the Budding Trees Moon, which begins at the time of the spring equinox, which usually occurs on March 21. The other moons of Wabun are the Frogs Return Moon and the Cornplanting Moon. The moons of Wabun are those of illumination and wisdom, as earth's children prepare to grow in their proper way.

Next come the moons of Shawnodese, Spirit Keeper of the South. These are the moons of rapid growth, when all the earth comes to flower and bears fruit for that year. The Strong Sun Moon is the first one of Shawnodese and begins on June 21, the time of the summer solstice. It is followed by the Ripe Berries Moon and the Harvest Moon. This is the season of growth and trust. Trust is necessary in this season, since growth is so rapid there isn't time to ponder progress.

The autumn is the season of Mudjekeewis, Spirit Keeper of the West. The first moon of Mudjekeewis is the Ducks Fly Moon, which begins on September 23, the day of the autumn equinox. It is followed by the Freeze Up Moon and the Long Snows Moon. These are the moons that bring us the time of introspection, the time of gathering strength to look within and contemplate the growth and progress made in the preceding seasons. These are the times to prepare for the season of resting and renewing to come.

Each moon has a particular totem, or emblem, in the mineral, plant and animal kingdoms, which shares characteristics with the people who are born during this time. From your starting totems you will learn about yourselves, at the same time you learn more about your other relations on the earth. People do have a responsibility to their totems, to give them respect, liking and gratitude for the lessons and the energies they contribute to the continuation of life on our common Earth Mother.

As you travel around the wheel, you should strive to learn as much as you can about the totems of any place that you stand, so you are always growing more knowledgeable about those who share the earth with you. When you stand in the place of a different moon, you have the capacity to take on the characteristics of the totems for that moon and to learn from them, as well as from your fellow two-leggeds. The more you are willing to learn, the further you can travel on your journey around the Medicine Wheel.

Remember as you read of the moons that not all people will have all of the same characteristics, even though they share the same moon and totems. All travel the wheel at their own speed. It is possible, during the time you stand at one position, to sometimes have moods or phases that seem more fitting to those of another moon. These can remind you of positions

---

through which you have passed or give you hints of the places you'll be traveling to next. The important message of the Medicine Wheel is that you allow yourself to keep traveling, rather than tying yourself to one position and blocking your energies from growing and changing.

Earth Renewal Moon (Snow Goose)
December 22 – January 19

People born under the Earth Renewal Moon, the first moon of the year, have the snow goose as their totem in the animal kingdom, the birch tree as their totem in the plant kingdom and the quartz as their totem in the mineral kingdom. Their color is white, and they are of the Turtle elemental clan. They are born between December 22 and January 19.

To understand those of the Snow Goose, let us look at their totems in the other realms of creation on the earth. Quartz, their mineral totem, is one of the most common and widespread elements on the earth. Quartz, which is composed of silicon dioxide, is a fairly hard mineral, with a vitreous luster. It can come in almost any color, but white or clear quartz is most common. This is the color of quartz associated with Snow Goose people. In olden times people believed that quartz was permanently frozen ice because of the cool feel it has. This theory was given more credence because you can sometimes find quartz that has a drop of water frozen within it, which was captured inside the mineral as it formed, and can never evaporate unless the mineral is broken. Crystal is the Greek word for ice. Because of its resemblance to ice, quartz was thought to ward off thirst. Even in this century Boy Scout manuals told young men to suck on quartz if they were thirsty.

Quartz is a power stone. We use it today in radio, radar, television, ultrasonics, and other fields as a transmitting force. It is said that, in crystal form, quartz had other powers to transmit, or aid in transmitting, powers that we don't have much knowledge of today. Often the scepters that kings and nobles carried had quartz crystals at their heads. So did the magic wands used by magicians. Some people claim that the destruction of Atlantis came about because of the misuse of quartz crystals, which, prior to that time, had been used to provide most of the energy used by the Atlanteans. Crystal balls, used by seers to determine the future, were made of quartz. Crystal bowls, used to see the future by gazing into water and to bring about rain, are another example of the magical use of this mineral. Tribes in Australia used quartz in their rain-making ceremonies. Tribes in the United States used quartz for many of the same purposes that ancients in all parts of the world did.

From the crystal, people of the Snow Goose can learn of their own powers to see things clearly and to let the energies of the universe flow through them. If Snow Goose people can keep themselves clear and fluid, they can act as receivers and transmitters for the great powers of the universe, the same as their mineral totem does. Snow Goose people have the cool exterior of quartz, which makes them appear reserved and unaffectionate to those around them. However, like their mineral, they will warm up, after a time, if those close to them pour their own warmth and energy into them. People of the Snow Goose will never melt to the point where they will become gushy or overly sentimental, but they can learn to reflect a steady warmth and light to those around them. The power of these people, like the power of the quartz, comes from their ability to accurately receive and transmit. Because this power can be a great one, it carries with it the potential seed of its own destruction, and, improperly used, this power can seriously hurt Snow Goose people, and many of those around them, much as the crystals are alleged to have destroyed Atlantis. From the quartz Snow Goose people can learn of their powers and of the caution they must use in exercising it. They can learn that they must not become too hard in their views or philosophies or, like quartz, they will crack into irregular pieces. By holding and being with quartz crystals, they can learn secrets that will come to them in no other way.

The plant totem of the people of the Snow Goose is the birch tree, one of the most ancient and abundant of trees. The birch is a stately and beautiful tree, sometimes reaching heights of forty-five or fifty feet. The bark can be white, yellow, brown or almost black. When the trees are young, the trunk is smooth. As they mature it becomes marked with its characteristic lines. The leaves of the tree are simple, bright green and serrated. It has long, hanging flowers, which are sometimes quite large. Birch is found in woodlands from the Arctic Circle to Florida and Texas.

In the old days most parts of the tree were used by Native people in the United States. The bark was used for writing, and some of the most important messages from the traditional people are preserved on birch bark scrolls. The sap of the tree was used as a beverage and a syrup. Yellow birch sap was combined with sassafras to make a drink similar to root beer. The bark and leaves were made into teas, which were used to help cure digestive problems and problems of the kidneys and bladder. Salicylic acid, the predecessor of aspirin, was extracted from its inner bark. Externally, the tea was regarded as helpful for skin conditions and swellings.

In woodland areas the leaves of the birch tree were sometimes placed on the hot rocks during sweat baths so their vapor could help to cleanse the body of any problems it might have and to get rid of excess static electricity. Branches of the birch were also bound together and used, during the sweats, to thrash the body, to improve circulation and help to expel any toxins.

Native people used to drag a birch branch around after planting to activate the microorganisms in the soil. The roots of the birch also activate compost piles, so it is good to place your compost under birch trees if available.

Like the birch, Snow Goose folks have a stately air about them, which hints at knowledge of ancient traditions and lost wisdoms. When Snow Goose people are allowing their energies to flow well, they will often receive information about such traditions and wisdom from the universal sources that can transmit to them. Because of this part of their nature, Snow Goose people have a real respect for tradition. While they know that changes must come, they feel that they should come in an orderly fashion that shows respect for the ways of older times. Once a tradition has become part of their lives—whether of religious ritual or family ways of doing things—they find it extremely difficult to break away from it. More than people of most other signs they have a real appreciation of tradition and ritual and a sense of the enrichment that these can bring to the fabric of human life. Like the scrolls made from the bark of their tree, Snow Goose people will often be human instruments to transmit important messages of the wisdoms of the past.

Snow Goose people can use the birch, literally and figuratively, to keep themselves free of anything toxic so that the energy running through them will remain positive enough to be of good value to them and to those they touch. Since Snow Goose people have the capacity to see things clearly, they often find themselves in positions where they counsel others. When they are doing so, they must be sure that they themselves are in a pure enough state to let the things that they see come through, free from any of their own prejudice or negativity. Like the birch, these folks can rid the air of any unnecessary static if they have taken care to keep themselves in a good state, where their energy can flow freely and purely.

A tea made from birch could be useful to people of this totem, as they have a tendency toward ailments of the digestive tract. Learning how to take a sweat, using birch leaves or branches, can help Snow Goose people keep in good shape, especially when they have pain or swelling of the bones, particularly those of the knees. Snow Goose people tend to have afflictions of the knees if they allow themselves to remain in an unbalanced state for too long.

From the snow goose, people of this totem can learn many things about their own nature, since those of the animal kingdom are closest to those of us in the human kingdom. The snow goose is a beautiful white bird, with black wing tips. The old scientific name for the snow goose was *Chen hyperborea,* which means "goose from beyond the north wind." The snow goose was named this because people did not know where these geese went when they migrated in the spring. Snow does help to govern the lives of these geese. They fly to their northern nesting grounds just as the snow and ice begin to melt in the spring, and they return when the snow begins to fall in the autumn.

Some species of the snow goose travel five thousand miles each year from their nesting grounds in the Canadian subarctic to the Gulf of Mexico and then back again. In their migration they fly in a loose V pattern, usually with an adult female as the lead goose. Each goose helps to break the air for those following. They fly slightly to one side of the goose ahead so that they can have unobstructed vision. The snow geese are very gregarious birds. When they are migrating, it is common to see twenty or thirty thousand birds all stopping to eat at the same site. At their nesting grounds, they show their respect for tradition by allowing the experienced nesters to have the first choice of nesting sites, and they keep their nests about twenty feet apart. They are cautious parents, being sure to cover their eggs with moss and grass to insulate them. Both the goose and the gander stay with the eggs during their incubation period. Baby geese have an egg tooth with which to break out of their egg, a process that takes twenty-four hours. They first make a crack through which they can breathe, then burst out, with a lot of energy, a day later. The parent birds stay with their goslings through their most intense period of growth. After the eggs hatch, the parents moult their primary feathers, which means that they are flightless for the first three to four weeks of their offspring's life. The goslings can fly when their slow developing wings reach the correct proportions, at about six weeks.

If you have ever been around domestic geese, you know about some of the habits of the snow goose. These birds are nitpickers, often spending hours picking mosquitoes or other insects off each other or anything that is around. They have a tugging instinct, which is manifest whenever they get a good hold on something, be it food, flesh or whatever. This tugging instinct is what is responsible for the "goose" that you might have someday received from a goose. Geese have much keener vision than humans, which helps them to be expert in their nit-picking and in their traveling. The sound of the snow goose is usually a "honk," but when several thousand honking geese are approaching, the sound can be mistaken for anything from a pack of wild dogs to yapping coyotes.

Snow geese make a strong impression on humans as they fly overhead, because of their beauty, their precision and their noise. Perhaps, more than anything, they stir our imaginations as we wonder where they are going and what always leads them to get there correctly. Many itchy-footed country people contracted this condition from letting their imaginations soar with these beautiful birds.

Like their totem, people of the Snow Goose have minds that are able to soar and cover vast distances. This is part of the reason that they are capable of having the amount of power that is possible for them. While, being of the Turtle clan, they are always grounded in the material world, their minds are capable of going to distant places, beyond Waboose, the North Wind. Snow Goose people are born under the first of the moons of Waboose, the Earth Renewal Moon, so, like the goose, their lives are governed by the snow. During the season of Waboose they are able to renew themselves by allowing their minds to fly while their bodies are at rest.

Like the goose, these folks have a respect for tradition and a real sense of obeying authority. While their minds might be breaking new frontiers, their conduct will always be very proper, bound in tradition and respectful of any authorities over them. These folks are also gregarious, like their totem, with a genuine liking for being around people. However, because of their reserve, they will often be around a lot of people in such an unobtrusive way that you might even forget that they are there at all. In groups they tend to make pleasant small talk, saying socially approved things, without ever letting people really get a look at who they are. It is difficult to break through the reserved exterior of people of the Snow Goose to find out what they are really like. Being of a discriminating nature, they are careful of who they allow to break through.

Snow Goose people, like their totem, are cautious parents, wanting always to be certain that their children are safe, well cared for and conforming to the modes of the day or the philosophies that the parents espouse. Snow Goose people like their homes and their children to be well organized, smooth running and as close to perfect as possible. As parents, these folks demand respect for their authority and like instant obedience in their children. They tend to be stern disciplinarians if they are crossed. Because of their reserve, they are not outwardly demonstrative to their children, expecting instead that the children will know of their love by the smooth way in which their lives are run. They might demand too much from their children, for too long a time, because of their sense of tradition and duty.

Children of the Snow Goose, like the goslings, are sometimes very quiet for the first period of their lives. They do the necessary tasks of living but don't seem to put forth a lot of effort otherwise. Like the gosling, though, at some point they decide to break through this self-imposed egg, and then they burst out with a lot of energy, demanding to be front and center on stage. The time at which this happens depends, of course, on the individual child.

The tendency to like the center stage continues in Snow Goose people throughout their lives, although it is often so masked in reserve that it is difficult to perceive. However, if Snow Goose people feel that they have control of the power coming through them and know how to act in front of other people, they will often be at center stage, sharing their clarity with whoever wishes to listen. When Snow Goose people are in balance, they can share a lot with others, and they can accomplish many different kinds of jobs in a good, thorough and neat way.

Like snow geese, people of this totem are nitpickers, in a figurative sense. Because they like neatness, and really would like all to be perfect around them, little things out of place in surroundings or people really bother them. They will spend hours telling friends how they can improve their natures, how they can make themselves more consistent. They are the type of people who will come into a house and dust the furniture off with their hands if it looks dirty, empty ashtrays, water droopy plants. They don't mean to insult your housekeeping. It just bothers them to be around things that are obviously, to them, left undone.

When Snow Goose people are out of balance, they, too, have a tugging instinct of sorts. They are quick to nip at the slightest provocation and they will try to tug the rug out from those around them. When they are in a bad mood, they tend to be jealous, skeptical, egotistical, arrogant and manipulative. They get bound up in their own melancholy feelings, and they want to drag everyone they know down with them. Because they are capable of letting their minds soar, because they can have much power coming through them, they are master manipulators when they set their minds to it. Since they also have the stability of the Turtle clan, they can enter into long schemes of subterfuge designed to revenge themselves against anyone they feel has slighted them. They are capable of playing very dirty ball if they feel that they have been slighted, insulted or otherwise hurt. And they can keep these tactics up for a long time, causing pain to those close to them and to anyone who mistakenly crosses their paths. Some Snow Goose people carry this on until their own power seems to turn against them in an effort to put them back on the proper path. During states like this they are very prone to digestive disturbances and to arthritis and rheumatism, especially of the knees.

Because of their Turtle clan traits—stability bordering on stub-bornness and a fear of anything except very gradual change—added to the persistence that is inherent in their natures, it is very difficult for Snow Goose people to turn themselves around when they are on an unbalanced course. Usually, it takes the prodding of their own power or help from someone who is equally powerful. Very often if they can learn to let their hair down, to be open, outward, even frivolous, they have taken the first step to regaining their balance.

The color of the Snow Goose people is the white of the snow itself, that magical form of water that floats down to earth, each flake in its own special form, making everything look fresh, sparkling, clean and new. White is the sum of all colors, which means that it contains within itself all of the other colors of the rainbow, the spectrum. It is considered to be the color of purity, of balance between all colors. It is said to be the color of perfection, of enlightenment, of evolution. It is invoked by many people to cover and shield themselves from any impure or negative vibrations that might be around them.

The color expresses the highest nature that people of this totem can aspire to. With their power, with their innate striving for perfection, people born under this totem can evolve themselves to a very high state if they learn how to balance all of the energies that flow through them. They can become pure in spirit.

This is also one of the most important lessons that being in this sign can give to people as they make their trip around the Medicine Wheel. It is here that they can renew themselves in such a way that they can balance all of the energy they have gathered while in other signs. It is here that they can find again the purity of spirit that will allow them to take as big steps as possible in their evolution.

The moon that governs these folks, the Earth Renewal Moon, the moon of the winter solstice, is the first moon of the year. It is the moon that brings people—as well as all the other children of Mother Earth—to their time of rest and renewal. As such, it does not cause as much emotional activity as some of the other moons of the year, and this is one of the reasons for the reserve that these people have. The moon in this sign does not act in such a way that it allows a lot of emotions to show. Rather, it is a moon that signals people to withdraw into themselves to rest, review the actions of the past year and prepare for the year to come.

People of the Snow Goose complement Flicker people, and they are most easily compatible with those who share the Turtle clan—Beaver and Bear folks—and also with those others of the Frog clan—Cougar and Snake people. When they are in a good balance, however, they are capable of getting along well with people of all of the other places on the Medicine Wheel.

Rest and Cleansing Moon (Otter)
January 20 – February 18

Those born during the second moon of the year, the Rest and Cleansing Moon, have the otter as their totem in the animal kingdom, the quaking aspen tree as their plant totem, and silver as their mineral totem. Their color is silver, and they are of the Butterfly elemental clan. According to the Medicine Wheel, the dates of birth of these people are January 20 to February 18.

People of this totem are like their mineral, silver, in that they tend to be precious to all who know them. Silver is one of the two most sought-after metals on the earth, and this seems to have been true since early times. Because of its malleability, its luster, its beauty and sheen, silver has long been considered one of the earth's most precious minerals. There are records of silver mines back in the early Incan period, as well as the early periods in other parts of the world. However, silver was not considered to be of great value on this continent until the Spaniards came here in their search for this mineral and, of course, for gold.

Silver has been used throughout the centuries as a measure of wealth. It is one of the most common minerals used in coins, jewelry and tableware in the homes of those who can afford it. Royalty had jewelry and crowns made of silver. Churches used it in their chalices. The rich had mirrors coated with silver.

Like their mineral, Otter people are very sought-after individuals. They make good friends and interesting companions. Like silver, they are malleable, able to adjust easily to most situations in which they find themselves. Because of their true liking for people, they, too, seem to have shine, a luster that makes them appear to be beautiful people, whatever their physical characteristics.

The color silver, which is the color of Otter people, is considered to have many magical properties. It is said that it is a silver cord that holds the soul to the body. Some religions believe that there are silver heavens above those of gold, that the former represent the highest vibration of pure spiritual power while the latter represent the vibration of love. Silver is the color associated with the Grandmother Moon, because the moon appears silver when we gaze at her. Because of this association, silver is considered to enhance the powers of the moon, the powers of perception, intuition and properly flowing emotional energy.

Otter people are said to have the capacity to possess certain magical qualities. They are usually very intuitive people if they allow their energies to flow properly. They have the capacity to become telepathic more easily than most other people. They are visionary people, always looking beyond what is obviously in front of them to what could be if others would awaken to their own higher natures. They have the capacity to allow pure spiritual power to flow through them if they have learned how to use their energies correctly.

Because of their tie with the moon, Otter people have the capacity to be very emotional, although they sometimes hide it. They feel things deeply, but they sometimes don't allow the deepest of their feelings to show through to other people. It is not that they are reserved. Rather, they prefer to keep things on a lighter note and not to trouble others with the depths of feeling they are capable of having. Some Otter people try to convert all this emotional depth into intellectual discussions. These folks love to have deep, penetrating, even heated discussions of whatever philosophy has currently taken their fancy. In these discussions they use all of the perception and intuition their ties to the moon give them to convert you to their way of thinking. It is very difficult to resist an Otter person in one of these sorts of discussions. Other Otter people use their emotional depth to pursue a wide variety of romantic partners, a pursuit in which they excel, due to the intensity of their feelings and their attractive natures. It is as difficult to resist an Otter person in romantic pursuit as it is to hold your own with one in an intellectual discussion.

The moon of this totem is the Rest and Cleansing Moon. It is the middle moon of Waboose, of the time of rest and renewal. Following the Earth Renewal Moon, when the sun begins to come back from the South, this moon brings a time of further rest for the earth and all of her children prior to the season when things begin to swing back into growth. This moon brings a time when people, having observed and renewed themselves, can cleanse themselves physically, mentally and emotionally to prepare for the times that are coming, when the pace of the seasons will make it more difficult to rest.

The plant totem for Otter people is the quaking aspen tree, also known as the white poplar and American aspen. Quaking aspen grow throughout the United States and Canada, from sea level to timberline. Their bark is a silvery brown, and their leaves are dark green with a silvery tint. When the gentle summer breezes blow through the leaves, they sound like tiny bells ringing. This trembling or quaking of the leaves is what gives this species of poplar its name. Its flowers are of catkin form, and the fruits are one-celled capsules containing a lot of small seeds with long tufts of silky hair that help their distribution by wind. The flowers of an individual tree are of a single sex. The bud of the tree is commonly called balm of Gilead.

According to Native American herbalists, the leaves, bark and buds of the tree traditionally have medicinal properties as a tonic and diuretic. The tea has often been used as a bitter tonic to aid in liver and digestive disturbances. It is also used as a relaxant capable of helping with hysteria and faintness and has also been used for hay fever. Native people used quaking aspen during their spring fast to clear their bodies of the winter's toxins.

Externally, the tea is considered to act as a tonic and conditioner when used weekly, and it has been used daily to help with serious skin conditions such as eczema, ulcers and burns. Some tribes here used the powder scraped from the bark as a deodorant, and they used scrapings of inner bark to treat cataracts.

Their plant totem can help Otter people learn to deliver the messages that come through them in a gentle and harmonious way, as the leaves of the tree do when they sing their song. It can also help them to learn that they have the capacity to sway gently with whatever winds are blowing and, by their swaying, allow the winds to blow through them and around them, without their ever breaking. By nature, Otter people are malleable, and this tree can show them that it is necessary for them to keep this quality if they want their energies to flow well.

The tea of the quaking aspen can help Otter people relax from the intensity that sometimes flows through them and can help them keep their internal organs in good condition so that they won't suffer from conditions of toxicity, which have a tendency to settle in their feet and ankles and give them problems. When their energy is allowed to flow smoothly, Otter people will usually be healthy, but, when they block the flow of energy, especially the energy of their emotions, they can suffer from a number of conditions that cause congestion in the body: hay fever, asthma, bronchitis. Quaking aspen can help prevent all of these.

The otter itself is considered by many naturalists to be one of the most pleasant and playful animals of the wild. There are two types of otters in this country, the river otter and the sea otter. The sea otter was almost extinct early in this century because its beautiful and durable fur was so sought after—bringing prices of up to $2,000 per pelt—that hunters massacred most of them. Prior to this time the sea otter was a friendly animal that would spend quite a bit of time basking on the shore. This made them an easy target for hunters, who would just come up and club them. Now the sea otter, which exists in the United States only off a small portion of northern California coastline, spends most of its time in the sea, eating, sleeping, sunning, playing, giving birth and raising its young all in the water. These otters have a shimmering, lustrous dark brown fur with silver hair, which is dense and fine. When mature they have a light-colored face with white whiskers. Like all otters they have webbed feet. They are as much at home in the water as the seal, usually choosing to live off a rocky piece of shoreline with abundant kelp beds, in which they relax, play and bear their young.

Otters range between three to five feet long, and between thirty-five and seventy pounds, sea otters being larger than those of the rivers. They are of the weasel family, although they act in such a considerate way that many people feel that this is an unfair classification for them. The river otter has a chocolate-brown coat with light gray underparts and throat.

The river otter, like his brother in the sea, depends on water for existence. They are found in most of the large lakes, marshes and rivers of the western United States and in many nations of the world. Their dens may be enlarged muskrat holes or other holes found in the riverbank. They have both underwater and overland entrances. Some otters make a wigwamlike den of reeds or cattails.

All otters have a voracious appetite, because of their fast metabolism. They eat fish, shellfish, insects, ducks and rodents. They have the ability to use rocks to open up their shellfish dinners, which makes them one of the few animals who have mastered the idea of utilizing tools. Otters have a wide vocabulary, which consists of chips, squeals, screeches, hiccoughs, chuckles and hisses when they are angry. Some of their calls carry for as far as a mile.

The otter is considered to be one of the most noble, curious and playful of wild animals. When they are not eating, hunting or sunning, they are most often playing. They make chutes down the riverbank and slide down them like children on a slide. They make them out of mud in summer and snow in winter. In the water they swim in groups, moving like dolphins. They play follow-the-leader, popping in and out of the water, and it is possible that otters at play started many legends of sea serpents in both the ocean and inland lakes.

Native people here recognized the power of this animal. In the Midewiwin, or Grand Medicine Society, of the Ojibwa people, most of the medicine bags of the sacred teachers were made from the skin of the otter. These bags had very great power.

Some naturalists, in speculating why the otter is so different from other members of the weasel family, have concluded that perhaps they felt that they had to set a good example to restore weasels to good grace in the eyes of the world. The otter has surely done so for some people.

Otters have warm and active homelives, with both parents assisting in raising the young. Their young stay with them longer than those of most wild animals. Otters are playful and ardent companions to each other, and a mate will mourn the death of his or her companion for several months.

With the otter as their animal totem, it is again easy to see why people of the Rest and Cleansing Moon are such sought-after companions. Like their totem, they are clever, bold, playful, helpful and gentle. They have a wide vocabulary and are as playful with words and philosophies as they are with other things.

People of this totem are like the otter in another important respect. They seem to feel that it is their duty to keep other humans in good grace in the eyes of the world. They are visionary and humanitarian, often spending much of their time and energy in searching for ways in which they can help their fellow humans. They truly enjoy being of service to people and dreaming of new ways in which they can serve. Because of their perceptive and intuitive natures, they are often successful in finding ways in which people can be of service to each other. If you examine charitable institutions, or alternative ways of living, you will often find an Otter person as the founder of them. This need to be of service is a large part of the nature of any Otter person, and, if they have not found ways to do it on a large scale, they will have found ways to do it on an individual basis.

If you have an Otter person as a friend, and you are in need of a sympathetic ear, a helping hand, even a financial loan, they will be there to give you as much as they can. But they are also practical, and if the loan is for something that they feel doesn't have much merit, they will first try to make you see your own impracticality. If they can't, they will often still give you money, even though they don't think you have a chance for success. Being patient, they will wait until you see the superior wisdom of their intuition. Because of their perception, these folks are quite capable of putting themselves in your place, wherever it may be, and honestly knowing what you are feeling at any time.

While Otter people, like their totem, are generally mild, loving and gentle, they do have the capacity to kick pretty strongly if they feel that you need a kick to get you back on the right road. Unless their energy is totally blocked and congested, they will not kick just for malice or spite. It is really infrequent to find a vengeful Otter person. They are, however, fearless and full of courage, and they are not afraid to take an unpopular position with their friends or their business companions, if they know that their position is right.

They do have latent, if not active, psychic abilities, stemming from their intuitive natures. Many Otter people use these abilities to make most of the everyday decisions of their lives, and then marvel at their own ability to make the right decision. Unless they have taken the time to study and develop these abilities, they do not even know where their power is coming from. Their visionary abilities also stem from these powers, and most Otter people are visionary to some extent, even if this only comes out in the fact that they often have powerful and prophetic dreams.

The major way in which Otter people can go wrong is if they become afraid of the power coming through them and attempt to block it. This can sometimes happen if they develop their intellectual natures so much that they can no longer keep in touch with their own intuitions. When this happens, they are very unhappy people, and they begin to lose many of the good qualities that they otherwise have. They also become prone to diseases of congestion. They must take care, if they are in a blocked period, to keep their adaptability, or they can crystallize in whatever blockage they have and cause their powers to cease flowing. If this happens, Otter people will begin making poor decisions in most areas of their lives, and their friends and family will have a hard time helping them because the Otter person, with his typical desire to keep things light, won't want to admit the root cause of his problem.

Being of the Butterfly clan enhances most of the qualities of Otter folks. However, with their own dreamy natures influenced by the sometimes flittering air spirits, Otter people have to make sure to develop their own practicality or they will have too many dreams to deal with, and none of them will become reality.

Like the otter, these folks make good, warm, gentle and caring parents. They spend enough time with their children to make them secure, yet they also take care to keep enough of their own space. They have the intuition and perception necessary to make good parents, knowing what their children need and when their needs are real. They generally are able to let go of their children as they grow, giving them the space to become their own people. They do have to guard against a tendency to want to put their own dreams onto their children, especially if they are in any period of blockage of their own emotional energy.

As children, Otter people sometimes seem to be in a faraway place, perhaps because their intuitive power allows them to remember the places they have been before their birth. It sometimes takes the experience of years before Otter people are able to become practical and adaptable and, during this time, they have to be guarded against potential harm since they are sometimes so far away they don't see the possibility that they might be in trouble. It also takes some years of living before Otter children become courageous and able to fearlessly be in the world. In this they are like the babies of the river otters who are afraid to swim until their parents are able to trick them into doing so. Once Otter people get in the flow of life, any problems that they may have as children will disappear.

As people travel around the wheel and come to the place of the Rest and Cleansing Moon they will have the opportunity to find and develop the perception and intuition in their own natures. They will often find untapped springs of gentleness and true concern for their fellow humans. During periods when people of other signs stand in the position of Otter people they will be able to formulate plans of how they can better learn to serve the Earth Mother and their fellow humans.

While people of the Otter can get along quite well with most everyone, their particular complement are those of the Sturgeon totem. Their easiest companionship will come from Deer and Raven people, their fellow Butterfly clan members, and from those of the Thunderbird clan, Red Hawk, Elk and, as mentioned before, Sturgeon people.

Big Winds Moon (Cougar)
February 19–March 20

◼◻◻ Those born during the Big Winds Moon, between February
◻◼◻ 19 and March 20, have the cougar as their animal totem,
the plantain as their plant totem and the turquoise as their
mineral totem. Their color is the blue-green of the turquoise, and
they belong to the Frog elemental clan.

The turquoise, their stone, is one of the oldest stones used for
adornment and protection. It was being mined in Egypt at least
six thousand years before the beginning of this Christian era and
on this continent at least one thousand years. Turquoise is a
hydrous aluminum phosphate, with copper or iron. It can range
from sky blue to bluish green to deep green. It has a waxy luster
and is one of the few jewels without a sheen that is so highly
prized. Turquoise is largely found in kidney-shaped masses
in veins within other rocks of almost any kind, although it is most
often found along with copper, iron or silver. Many of the stones
have veins, or matrixes, of these other ores running through
them.

Turquoise was referred to as the "skystone" by the Native
people. There is one old Indian legend that says that the sky is
blue because a golden spirit eagle sits on top of a turquoise
mountain and reflects the mountain's color up to the sky. Many
powers are attributed to the stone. It was believed in many places
that people wearing turquoise would never break their bones
because the turquoise would fracture instead, thus protecting the
wearer. It is because of this belief that horse's bridles, harnesses
and tails were decorated with turquoise to ensure that the animal
was even-footed.

In some countries turquoise was used as the stone in engage-
ment rings. People believed that the stone would remain blue
as long as the couple were faithful to each other, but would turn
green if either were untrue. That seems a fairly hard test for
anyone with oily skin, as turquoise is a very porous rock and will
change color because of contact with skin oil, or just about
any liquid.

Many Native people in the United States believed that turquoise
could keep its owner from injury or danger, and so they used it
in shields to turn aside weapons. Turquoise was also used
extensively both here and in Central and South America in
religious ceremonies and was carved into fetishes or inlaid into

---

other objects. Navajos used to throw turquoise into the river, with special prayers, as part of their rain-making ceremony. Apaches believed that turquoise could be found at the end of the rainbow. Other tribes would fasten a turquoise bead to a bow or arrow, believing that this would make the arrow always hit its target.

Like their stone, Cougar people have the possibility of having many powers that are outside of the ordinary. They have a lot of natural medicine that can make them adept at many of the mysteries of life and the universe.

Like the turquoise they can be people of the sky, initiates into many of the life processes that people of other totems do not know. But, like their stone, they have to be cut well to show their proper color. Without the right experiences of life, and without a willingness to do some real work on themselves, their natural powers don't develop but turn against them making them into moody, even melancholy people. This can happen to those who can see the mysteries of the sky but cannot see how to build a bridge from the earth to get there, while still functioning well on this plane.

Cougar people often have the power to be healers, and, like their stone, they will often be involved with various types of religions and their ceremonies. Being of the Frog clan, their minds have the ability to flow into many realms, and most Cougar people make use of this ability to search out whatever things of life they can. The mystical, magical realm is often more comfortable to these folks than any other. For this reason it is important that they are careful that they have grounded themselves in the earth, or are around others who are grounded, or they will sometimes travel into these other realms and not have the ability to bring themselves back.

The plant totem of the Cougar people is the plantain, a common herb which is a well-known healer. There are two hundred species of the herb, and they grow all over the world. The leaves all radiate from the base but, in some types, are broader than they are in others. They are dark green and have very visible lengthwise ribs. The flower of the plantain is a dull white and grows from six to eighteen inches high.

The whole plant is used as a healer. Natives here used it both internally and externally to cool and soothe as well as heal. It is a blood cleanser and helps to alleviate pain and reverse the effects of poison. It does wonders for healing either fresh or old sores, used either as a tea or a compress, and it is effective against stings and bites. It does the same thing for the inside of the body as it does for the outside, and so it has been used to heal ulcers of the stomach or intestine, inflammation of these areas, kidney and bladder trouble. As a bath or a strong tea used in compresses it will aid in most conditions of aches and pains.

It is useful for Cougar people to dip the leaves in vinegar, dry them overnight and place them on the feet before putting on their shoes, as plantain used in this way will help to relieve pain of the feet and legs, a pain that these folks are prone to have. Its soothing internal effect will help Cougar people to keep their internal organs in good condition when they are in melancholy states. In that condition they are prone to diseases caused by inflammation of the stomach and intestines, which often come about through worrying. Externally, plantain will help to cure any skin lesions caused by stress and worry.

Because plantain is so widely spread and well rooted in the earth, it can help Cougar people to learn about their own need to ground themselves in this environment before they reach too high for the sky.

The color of Cougar people is the blue-green of the turquoise. Blue represents the sky, as well as spiritual aspiration. It indicates a seeking, spiritual person, and one prone to self-imposed struggle and melancholy. In its purer color it connotes idealistic, selfless, artistic and spiritual feelings. It is said that the color of a seeker on the proper path is blue.

The green mixed with the blue is helpful to Cougar people, as it gives them a balance between spirit and personality, between the sky and the earth. Remembering to keep green as well as blue around them will help them to be serene and can help to restore and heal them when they are out of balance. Since Cougar people are spiritual by nature, they usually prefer a pure blue, but they should remember the benefits that adding green or using, instead, a green-blue will give to them. This is an especially useful color for them to wear or have around if they are doing healing work.

The animal totem for people of the Big Winds Moon is the

cougar, the lion of this continent. Unfortunately, our native lion has not been given the same respect as its African counterpart. The cougar has tended to be misunderstood and feared, and this has often resulted in its wanton slaughter. The cougar is also known as the mountain lion, puma, panther, screamer, painter and ghost cat. It is the largest member of the feline family on this continent usually measuring between seven to nine feet, and weighing 150 to 300 pounds. It is an unspotted cat, after it has left the kit stage, with a tawny tan to gray coat and lighter underparts. Its tail and ear tufts are tipped with brown or black fur, which never seems to stay still. The cougar has a handsome face and a round head with prominent whiskers.

The cougar is found in the western states, Florida, Canada and Mexico at this time. They used to be found all across the United States prior to the spread of this current civilization. Because of the treatment they have received at man's hands, they now largely inhabit steep canyon country or mountainous terrain. They make their dens in rocky caves, washout holes or thick brush.

Of all cats cougars are considered to be the best climbers. If pursued or hunting they can climb trees, although they prefer to stay on the ground. They are swift runners, although they are not good at lengthy long-distance runs. They cover large individual territories, but their social structure does not allow these territories to overlap. They are careful to mark their ranges so other cougars do not intrude. Cougars have a harsh, high-pitched scream which can be quite terrifying, but it is seldom heard. Cougars tend to be silent unless they are cornered and then they growl, snarl and spit.

Cougars are hunters, with deer being the mainstay of their diet, although they will eat other small animals. They like the chase of the hunt, and often join efforts with their mate or relations to obtain better results. One cougar will chase the animal, while the other waits in ambush. They do not hunt for more food than they eat. They only turn to livestock when their natural food supplies have been so depleted that they have no choice. The cougar is one of the most expert of wild hunters, because of his speed, power and endurance. In his lithe and graceful way the cougar will move in circles through his territory so swiftly and silently that he was sometimes called the "sneak cat." He is a patient hunter, sometimes making many approaches before he gets into his desired position. Cougars have sometimes waited a day and a night on a ledge or limb to have a chance to make their meat. Female cougars are better hunters than the males.

One nasty rumor about the cougar is that it would hunt humans. There is no documented case of a cougar who was healthy ever having done so. They do, however, like to follow humans, but this is out of curiosity, natural to felines, not out of hunger.

When cougars mate, the female is often the aggressor. She will chase after the male of her choice and then give him a few swats to get his attention. When he reciprocates, they wrestle for a while before sealing the relationship. Male cougars do not have much to do with raising the young kits. Most litters are born in the spring and consist of only two kits. The mother cougar is very loving and devoted to her kits, and she will protect them against anything that threatens them, whether a wild predator or a man hunting with a pack of hounds. It is possible for a cougar to outfight a dozen hound dogs on the ground, but the hounds usually tree the animal so that their master can shoot it.

People who have the cougar as their animal totem share many traits with this kingly cat. They like to keep to themselves, in the high territory of their own minds and spirits, because they often feel that they have been hurt at the hands of their fellow humans. They are very sensitive people, and they can be easily hurt, even by chance remarks with no harmful intentions. Like the cougar, they like to have their own den, a place to which they can retreat for contemplation and self-analysis. Like their totem, they are good climbers, although most of their climbs are ones of the mind and spirit rather than physical ones.

In their minds they are swift runners, capable of going to distant realms where few others travel. Cougar people need to have their own territory. This is essential to their well-being and balance. Without the proper spiritual territory in which to travel, they become moody and dissatisfied individuals. With the proper direction, they can be among the most productive of humans.

Like their totem, Cougar people also have the tendency to mark their territory, whether it is of philosophy, of business or of relationships. Once this is marked they do not like others to intrude into it, without their invitation, and they will be hurt if other people try to do so. They seem to be especially wary of other people of their own totem coming into their territory, perhaps because, more than others, they are aware of the potential power that they share.

Cougar people are often silent, especially about the things that they really feel. They find it easy, when they are in good balance, to initiate the kind of conversation that makes other people feel comfortable, but they will not reveal any of their true selves until they are sure of those around them. Because of the intuitiveness that comes from their ability to pierce other realms, they can easily sense what kind of talk and actions will make others feel comfortable, and they will usually make the effort to do this for other people, as they are gentle souls who are capable of truly liking others.

Because Cougar people tend to keep silent on many of their deepest feelings, they often feel cut off from people, as though they are outsiders that others are not capable of understanding. They often repress these feelings for a long time, sometimes for their whole lives. If they are around others they trust enough and these feelings begin to surface, they can come out in a scream of emotion that can be terrifying both for Cougar people and for their friends. Cougar folks must learn to find others they trust enough to let their feelings come out, even if it is temporarily frightening, for they will never find their true spiritual expression if they are weighted down by a lifetime's worth of suppressed emotion. This blocked energy is what often plunges them into depths of depression and melancholia and keeps them from grounding themselves so that they are capable of successfully reaching for the sky. Fear of their repressed emotion also can keep them from being able to make clear decisions, a trait that sometimes makes them seem indecisive.

Like their totem, Cougar people are hunters but, again, what they are hunting is most often spiritual development, not anything on the material plane. They, too, enjoy the chase of the hunt and will often enjoy hunting these things with people who have proven themselves to be true friends and sincere seekers. A balanced Cougar person is as lithe and graceful, both spiritually and physically, as his totem. Cougar people are also intelligent enough to know that they have to be patient in order to successfully hunt the things that they are seeking. They will usually try a number of approaches before settling on the position that they take. This trait, too, tends to earn them the "indecisive" label.

In relationships between two Cougar people, the female, like her totem, will be the aggressor. She has to be or the relationship will never get started. Outside of Cougar relationships, however, the female Cougar person will passively wait for the other person to take the lead. This is true of the Cougar male in other relationships also. Cougar people have to be coaxed and teased into relating to someone else, then they need to be constantly assured that the other person really wants to continue the relationship. While Cougar people can learn to be secure in the correct spiritual realm, they will always need reassurance that they are doing the proper thing in the material realm.

The insecurities and moodiness that Cougar people sometimes have are intensified by their membership in the Frog clan. Frog clan people are sensitive to the shifting flow of human emotions, and this additional sensitivity makes Cougar people even more aware of the potential pitfalls of any human relationship. On the positive side, their membership in this clan increases Cougar people's ability to know and flow with the creative and unifying energies of the universe.

Cougar men do not have an easy time with parenthood. They find it hard to relate to the very physical demands that a child makes upon its parents. While they can truly love their children, they find it difficult to express this love. Cougar women have a little bit easier time of it, since, like the cougar, they have a protective and devoted attitude toward their children while they are young and need them. As the children get older, however, this strong maternal instinct tends to dissipate as the mother wants to get on about her own business of exploring the spiritual realms with which she is most comfortable.

Cougar children need a lot of love and protection, as they are dreamy and still very much in the realms from which they have come. They need to be grounded as quickly as they can so that they are capable of surviving their own childhoods. They should also be taught to express whatever emotions they can at this age, as it will make it easier for them to continue doing so as they grow older. They are bright, intuitive and gentle children. You are just not sure that they are always hearing what you are saying to them, and you're probably correct.

Cougar children are very creative. You don't need to buy them a lot of toys, as they can make a toy out of anything that takes their fancy. This creativity does continue as Cougar people mature, and, as long as they do keep grounded, they can be excellent artists in any medium. Often this creativity will come out in their spiritual searches as well as in artistic form.

When Cougar people lose their balance, they can be very fierce toward anyone they feel has wounded them. When they feel cornered, they will unsheath their claws and really put up a remarkable fight. Sometimes fighting serves a constructive purpose for them, as it is one way they can express some of the emotions that they tend to repress. It can often get them out of one of their melancholy times. But it can also hurt the others in the battle, sometimes more seriously than the Cougar people think.

The moon of the Cougar totem is the Big Winds Moon, a moon of mystery when the season is almost ready to turn and the winds blow freely from all directions. It is a time of rapidly changing energies as all of earth's children prepare for the time of new growth that follows the season of rest. Being born under this moon intensifies the mysterious and restless side of the Cougar nature. It increases the ability they have to deal with the energies coming through them.

This is the third moon of Waboose, Spirit Keeper of the North. Her gift of purity helps Cougar people to retain their spiritual purity despite any problems they have on the material plane. Her gift of renewal helps them to bounce back from even their most severe bouts of melancholia.

Cougar people complement those of the Brown Bear and find easiest compatibility with their fellow Frog clan members, those of the Flicker and Snake; and with the others of the Turtle clan, those of the Beaver and Snow Goose. When they are in good balance, they do, however, find it easy to relate to most people, at least on a superficial level. They do need to watch how they relate to Deer people, as they sometimes can be unconsciously vicious to them, as the cougar is to mule deer.

When people of other signs find themselves in this position during their trip around the wheel, they will experience as much spiritual energy as they are capable of handling, and sometimes a little more. In this, they will experience the feelings of impending chaos that often stalk those of the Cougar, making it a difficult task for them to learn to truly be in balance. People traveling through this position will also have the opportunity to pierce through realms that are closed to them at other times.

Budding Trees Moon (Red Hawk)
March 21–April 19

Those born in the period of the Budding Trees Moon, the first moon of Wabun of the East, have the fire opal as their mineral totem, the dandelion as their plant totem and the red hawk as their animal totem. Their dates of birth fall between March 21 and April 19. Their color is yellow, and they are the first of the Thunderbird clan people.

Like quartz, opal is composed of silicon dioxide, but it has water added to it. Opal is found in sedimentary rock and in cavities in volcanic rock. It is also found near hot spring deposits and can be the replacement material in petrified wood. Opal comes in practically all tints and has a glassy to waxy luster. Opal is porous so it can be easily stained. It can fracture easily, sometimes for no apparent reason, and it also has a tendency to lose its water. Fire opals with small, evenly distributed flashes of light are known as pin fire opals; and those with regular squarish formations are known as harlequins. Harlequins are thought to be the rarest and most beautiful variety.

Like turquoise, opal has been used by people since very early times. The opal was considered to be the symbol of hope and was also thought to render its wearer invisible at times when he did not wish to be seen. Because of the fire in the stone, which can resemble the sunrise, sunset or the moonrise, the stone was connected with the powers of the sun, the moon and of fire.

In Europe the opal had an interesting history, with most of the above mentioned attributes associated with it in early times. In Rome it was known as the noble stone, and it is reported to have been so highly valued by one Roman senator that he went into exile rather than give his opal to Marc Antony, who wanted it for Cleopatra. Opals are among the crown jewels of France and were owned by the Imperial Cabinet of Vienna. However, a story written in England during the last century pictured the opal as a stone possessing an evil power, and, following that time, the opal was considered to be unlucky, in English-speaking countries, until it began to be in vogue again in the recent past.

Opals are found in this country in almost all areas, although those considered to be precious opals have only been found in the Northwest. Hungary, Mexico and Australia are the most fertile sources of the stones. While some areas produce opals of various types, generally each district produces a singular color of the mineral with its own particular fires and hues. Most black opals come from Australia, while the milky white or translucent ones come from Mexico. Some opals lose their fire if exposed to water, while others lose it if they are not exposed to water. If you have some transparent fire opals and allow them to sift through your fingers, they appear like a shower of shooting stars.

Like their mineral totem, Red Hawk people can often be found near hot spots or places of pressure either in the literal or figurative sense. Red Hawk people like the sun and warmth, and they also like to be in active situations which can utilize their intense mental, physical and emotional energy. Like their stone, they are porous, and their spirits can be easily stained if they associate themselves with the wrong ideas or people. They are usually open people, willing to listen to any new ideas or philosophies, and sometimes they accept things that later prove harmful for them. When they find themselves in the wrong situations or under too much strain, they can fracture, like their stone, and lose the life vitality that usually gives them their fire and sparkle.

Red Hawk people, like the opal, can be of the type that sparkle constantly with small pin fires of energy, or they can be ones who only flash sometimes when the fires of vitality spring up in them, or they can be harlequins, with regular fire formations that glow constantly. Which they are depends on how much they have learned about harnessing and utilizing the fire of the life force that flows easily through them. It is rare to find ones who have succeeded in controlling their energy to the point where it is always available to them. This type of Red Hawk person is very valuable, as they can not only begin projects but also keep them going with the strength of their energy.

Red Hawk people, like the opal, are often the symbol of hope for any new idea that is struggling to be born. They are catalysts, capable of making an idea into a reality. These folks, like their stone, have a direct connection with the sun, and with fire, a connection that is strengthened because they are of the Thunder-bird clan. Their connection with the moon, or their emotions, is more difficult for them to deal with, but very essential if they are going to be successful in learning to use their own energies well. The fire in Red Hawk people comes from their emotions, which move even faster than those of most other people. But, being people who favor things that appear clear, they often fear the complexities of their own and other people's emotions.

Being of the Budding Trees Moon, the first moon of the spring, the moon of the spring equinox, gives Red Hawk people a further boost in energy levels. This is the moon that governs one of the most rapid times of growth for all of earth's children, and so it brings with it an energy of rapid growth and change. This helps to give Red Hawk people their apparent adaptability, an ability to grow quickly from one philosophy or project to another.

Dandelion, the plant totem of the Red Hawk people, is probably a familiar plant to most people and one that does not necessarily conjure up happy pictures to those who like smooth, green, grassy front lawns. For any who don't know it, dandelion is a shiny green rosette of tooth-edged leaves. The flower stem, which grows to six inches or more in height, bears a single yellow flower, which becomes a ball of white fuzz when the seeds are formed—a ball that disperses and goes off with the wind. The root and stem yield a milky liquid when cut. While the root is the official medicinal part, the whole herb is very useful.

Rather than poisoning their dandelions, gardeners should wait until they are in flower and then pluck them up, root and all. The root can be dried and used as a coffee substitute or an herbal remedy, and the greens can be cooked as a potherb. The greens, especially when they are older, do have a bitter taste, as well as a slight narcotic property. In preparing them it is good to soak them in salted water for about half an hour before using, or to cook them in several waters, always throwing out the previous one. Dandelion greens contain almost seven times the amount of vitamin A per ounce as carrots or lettuce, plus goodly amounts of vitamins B, C, and G, calcium, phosphorus, iron and natural sodium, which helps to purify and alkalize the bloodstream.

Native healers here, as well as in most other parts of the world, used dandelion root as a tonic that would help to open and cleanse all of the eliminative organs of the body. It also helps to soothe and relax these organs and your body in general. They also used dandelion as a diuretic and an agent to balance the blood sugar level in the body. Some Native people used the roots as a sedative.

Like the dandelion, Red Hawk people have the tendency to pop up all over the place, since they are usually flying from one project to another. This habit doesn't endear them to people who find it hard to deal with their energy level, and don't understand the benefits that a Red Hawk person can bring to things that interest them. All the energy of Red Hawk people, like all of the parts of the dandelion, can be useful to people who know how to help them channel it. Like their herb, they are a treasure-house of useful things to those who take the time to understand them.

Red Hawk people have the property of opening, and beginning to cleanse, the things, ideas and people that they touch. Since they are so forthright themselves, they do not like to find insincerity or manipulation in others, and they will speak their minds if they feel that these qualities are there. Red Hawk people are sincere, and often right in what they see. Those who can listen to what they have to say find that the things they learn give them an impetus toward opening up their own minds and emotions. Opening in this way is the first step toward cleansing any negative qualities out of yourself.

Red Hawk people can benefit from the soothing, relaxing qualities of the dandelion, as they often find it difficult to turn off their energy when their work for the day is completed. Dandelion, mixed with other herbs, might be useful for them in clearing up congestion of the head, with which they are often afflicted. Red Hawk people, since they are headstrong, often have problems with diseases of the head. They have a tendency to hit their heads accidentally a lot more frequently than other people, perhaps because they sometimes tend to fly into things too quickly, without taking the time to look them over.

In this way they are like their animal totem, the red-tailed hawk. The red-tailed hawk is of the genus *Buteo,* which means a hawk with a broad wing span and a fan-shaped tail. The adult is the only hawk with a red tail. It is a large hawk, often two feet long with a wing span of up to four and one-half feet. When these hawks are immature, they have a brown body with their underparts streaked with brown. Their tail is brown above and barred with brown below. It becomes red as they mature. Adult hawks have a light phase in which the chest, throat and stomach are usually white, streaked with brown. During their dark phase they are brownish black throughout their bodies. In both of these phases the wide, rounded tail is reddish brown, and easy to see when they are in flight. The red-tailed hawk is also called the chicken hawk, an unfair name which has caused their slaughter by farmers who felt that they were stealing their poultry. In one study done in the last century it was discovered that poultry only comprised 10 percent of the hawks' food, which largely consisted of mice, gophers, squirrels, rabbits and insects. When the hawks were killed off, the rodents often destroyed the crops, a fitting example of natural justice. The red-tailed hawk seems to have a particular fondness for rattlesnake meat. Luckily, they have scaled, not feathered, legs, which protects them against snakebite. They are not, however, immune to snake venom, which sometimes makes them the victim rather than the victor when they go after their favorite meat. When they capture a snake, they immediately tear the head off, to protect themselves.

Red-tailed hawks are frequently attacked by crows, magpies, owls, other hawks and songbirds in territorial disputes, but these attacks do not frequently end in injury. Perhaps you have seen smaller birds attacking hawks and other predatory birds when they are in flight. At these times the smaller birds have the advantage of being quicker, and they know that they cannot be captured as long as they are above their bigger brothers. Red-tailed hawks can live up to fourteen years. They usually nest in a tall tree, cactus or yucca or on the face of a cliff. They have two to three eggs in the spring, white, lightly splotched with brown. Both parents help in raising the young, and they often return for years to the same nest. Hawks used to be found all over the country, but now largely in the western states, Mexico and Canada. However, red-tailed hawks are adaptable and can be found almost anywhere. Their voice in flight can sound like steam escaping from a kettle, a throaty *skeeeer*. Up closer it sounds more like *guh-runk*.

Red-tailed hawks are magnificent in flight. They soar and circle for long periods, sometimes twisting their tail at an angle to their body. It is a joy to watch them on a windy day riding the currents with obvious gusto. They can be real acrobats, especially when they are mating. They can touch their mates in midair or drop several thousand feet in one dive.

Along with the eagle, the bird of the East, red-tailed hawks are very special birds to Native people. Those of the Pueblo societies referred to them as red eagles and considered that they, like the eagle, had a special connection with the sky and the sun. Because the birds can fly so high and see the earth so clearly from their heights, feathers from them were often used ceremonially to carry prayers to the sun and beyond, to the Creator. Hawk feathers, as well as eagle, were also used in healing ceremonies and, in the Southwest, in ceremonies to pray for rain. Hawk and eagle feathers are still used in most of these ways by Native people today, as well as in fans and bustles for dancing. To the Ojibwa and some other peoples, the Red-tailed Hawk clan was one of the leadership clans, and its members were credited with having the gifts of deliberation and foresight.

Like the red-tailed hawk, people born during the Budding Trees Moon are often large people, in spirit if not in body, and they have the capacity to spread their wings to a great width. Red Hawk people, like their bird, are hunters, although what they hunt out are new things to do, new projects to begin, new philosophies to explore. These folks tend to have light and dark phases. During the former they are joyful and open to everything. While in the latter, they want to fly off to be alone someplace to discover what has made the world seem wrong to them.

Red Hawk people tend to be fearless, often going after what they see as the rattlesnakes of the world with little regard for their own safety. As mentioned earlier, these folks have little or no patience with people they see as hypocritical or unjust. They will clearly tell such people what they see about them, whether or not the other person wishes to listen. Sometimes they grapple with snakes too large for them to handle, and, in this instance, they, too, can end up as the victim rather than victor. In many old mythologies the snake is considered to represent the underworld, while the eagle or hawk represents the zenith, although this is not a completely proper interpretation of these symbols. Nonetheless, since these two animals have often been pictured as antagonists, Red Hawk and Snake people sometimes have a difficult time reaching an understanding with each other unless both have grown to the point where they can correctly understand their symbolism, and how they can complement as well as antagonize each other.

As the hawk tears off the head of the snake to protect itself, so Red Hawk people will tear off the heads of anyone they see as potential enemies. They truly act as though the best defense is a good offense. When they are angry, their comments, like talons, can really sting. As the hawk is often attacked in flight by smaller birds, so Red Hawk people are attacked by people who won't understand them or their forthright energy when they are soaring off on the wings of a fresh idea or project. However, these attacks usually don't end in injury and sometimes precipitate conversations that can clear up misunderstandings on either part. If you have learned to love or trust your Red Hawk friends, you will find that they are truly beautiful to watch when they are in flight, just as their animal totem is. At these times the energy of life flows through and around them so completely that you can often find yourself flying, too. When they are in this stage of energy, they can be real acrobats with their minds and spirits, clearly seeing things of life that are often clouded from view.

The sky is the realm of Red Hawk people. From their flights there they are able to see clearly how things should be on earth. This is their strength: to be able to get new things begun in a good way, or established things back on their proper path. They truly want to do good and to see things unfold in their best possible way. They are natural optimists, strong-willed and energetic in their determination to set things right. They are independent people, and thinkers, and they are always sincere about what they think and feel. While their actions sometimes appear rash, they usually have carefully deliberated within themselves before deciding to act. Their natures in many ways are as fresh and open as that of a child just learning to talk. However, like a child, they often don't have a long concentration span, and they tire of something when it has just begun to work. They don't feel they need to stay around to be sure it is really working. To balance their energies they need to learn to have more patience and stability.

Like the feathers of their totem, they do have the ability to soar high in the sky and communicate with the Creator spirit. However, they generally expend most of their energy seeing how things should be on earth, and forget that they have this ability, too. They must learn to nurture and use this gift before they will be successful in truly balancing their energies.

Because of their clear sight, foresight and energy, Red Hawk people make good leaders when they have learned to channel their energy and to stay with something as long as it needs them. Once they have learned to direct the energy coming through them, they can succeed at most anything that they wish to, but that process of learning is often a long and painful one for them, and one that can take them through many dark phases of feeling.

Yellow is the color of Red Hawk people, the yellow of the spring sun and the dandelion flower. This color helps them by stimulating their intense intelligence and helping them to turn thinking into wisdom. It helps them to be more receptive and to maintain their usual friendliness, good health and well-being. Red Hawk people, other than bumping their heads a lot, tend to be physically strong and can maintain good health if they remember to take proper care of themselves.

Being of the Thunderbird clan intensifies most of the natural traits of Red Hawk people and gives them even more energy and penetration than they would otherwise have. More than people of the other totems of this clan they must guard against blazing so brightly at one point that they burn themselves out. They must learn to temper the energy their clan membership gives them, so the fire within them can always bring warmth and light to the things that they touch.

Being born under the first moon of Wabun, the Spirit Keeper of the East, tempers the energy of Red Hawk people with the wisdom Wabun brings. It also helps them channel their energy toward finding ways to bring about spiritual evolution in themselves and in others.

As children these folks are headstrong and sometimes difficult to control. They have an even higher level of energy than adults of this totem do, and it can be a real job to keep up with them. They are friendly, open, intelligent and usually healthy if they can be made to relax occasionally. Otherwise they are prone to colic, colds and other ailments caused by problems with the nerves or the head.

Red Hawk people go into parenthood as enthusiastically as they do anything else. If their energy is not channeled well, however, they will lose interest in it just as quickly, and the children will be left to fend for themselves, at least on an emotional level, while the parent is off exploring new things that interest him or her. They will always be friendly and sincere with their children and quick to correct them if they see them taking a wrong turn. They will tend to treat their children much as they treat any of their other friends, which sometimes means that their children lack the special emotional support that they need from parents.

Being naturally friendly and gregarious, Red Hawk people can get along with anyone, but they find friendships with other Thunderbird people, those of the Sturgeon and Elk, and with Butterfly people, those of the Deer, Raven and Otter, particularly fulfilling. Their complement is the Raven totem.

As people from the other starting places on the wheel travel through the position of the Red Hawk people, they will find new depths of energy in themselves and the ability to see and work clearly with things on this earth plane. They may discover resources for leadership within themselves that they never knew existed.

Frogs Return Moon (Beaver)
April 20–May 20

People born during the Frogs Return Moon, April 20 to May 20, have the beaver as their totem in the animal kingdom, the blue camas as their totem in the plant kingdom and the chrysocolla as their totem in the mineral kingdom. Their color is blue, and they are of the Turtle elemental clan.

Their stone, the chrysocolla, is similar, in many ways, to the turquoise. It is often found as a by-product of the copper mining process, as is the turquoise. Chrysocolla is a hydrous copper silicate. It ranges from a true green to greenish blue to a true blue color. It has a shining, glassy luster and, at the same time, an earthy look to the stone. Chrysocolla has the property of sticking to the tongue, and this is often the way it is distinguished.

Like turquoise, chrysocolla has been used for adornment since early times, although it is not as valued as turquoise. Its startling blue color, when it is found in this shade, mixed with its earthy luster, has given it a reputation of being a stone that has the possibility of helping its wearer to balance the elements of earth and sky within himself. It is considered a stone of good medicine that will help to bring luck and good health to its owner. It is also considered a stone that can purify the body, heart, mind and spirit. It has been used in earlier times, and today, to make fetishes or nuggets which have and will retain the color that is often associated with pure turquoise. It tends to retain its original color more than turquoise will.

From this stone Beaver people can learn to combine within themselves the powers of the earth and the sky. Most Beaver people, by their natures and by their membership in the Turtle clan, are very rooted in the earth, sometimes too rooted. They can find happiness by living well on the earth level without ever looking skyward to see what lessons there are for them in this realm. The beautiful blue shade of the chrysocolla can be an especially helpful reminder to them that, to be balanced, they must look upward as well, to find what is there for them to learn in the other realms of living.

Like their stone, Beaver people appear lucky, although often their apparent luck comes about as the result of hard work, and a practicality that lets them know when to be at the right place at the right time. They also have strong bodies and can enjoy good health, especially if they wear their stone, as long as they remember to curb their tendency to overindulge. These folks, like chrysocolla, will retain their original color, or nature, unless something really drastic happens to make them change. They are very stable people, and they are most comfortable being in situations that allow them to retain whatever stability that they can. It is unusual to find people of the Beaver totem who will throw knapsacks on their backs unless they are traveling through another position on the wheel. When they travel or change their environments, they like to do so in as systematic a way as possible. They just feel more comfortable having at least some familiar things around them.

This unchanging part of their nature, which reflects a quality of their mineral, makes these folks very good friends to have. Once they decide that they are your friend, they will not easily change their minds. They are loyal associates to have and ones that can bring stability to people or projects of a more mercurial nature.

Like chrysocolla, Beaver people have an ability to bring a feeling of purity to things and people that they touch. This comes from their loyalty, their stability and their willingness to treat friendships and other relationships in a way that seems so clean and sparkling by current standards that it feels like it comes from a purer time and place.

The plant associated with people of this totem is the blue camas, a wild member of the lily family. Several types of camas grow in this country, and it is essential to differentiate between them. In the East is wild hyacinth, or squills, which looks much like the western blue camas except that it is smaller and has paler blue flowers. Blue camas has basal, grasslike leaves, eight to fifteen inches long. The flowers, which appear in early May, are a brilliant blue. They grow on a single stalk and have three sepals and three petals. The plant can grow to three feet, but usually stops at two.

There is another type of camas, which usually grows near blue camas. The leaves, stem and bulbs look just like those of blue camas, but it has yellow or greenish-white flowers. This is known as death camas and should never be eaten, as it will make you very sick, or worse, depending on the quantity ingested. It is said that the bulbs and leaves of death camas will leave a burning sensation when touched to the tongue. To be safe it is best to dig up camas bulbs when the plants are in flower, although the bulb, which looks like a small onion, would be bigger if left until the end of the summer.

Blue camas was a staple food for Native people in many parts of the United States. They would mark the edible plants with strips of bark when they were in flower and then go back to pick the bulbs when they had reached optimum size. Native people cooked the bulbs by digging a hole, lining the bottom and sides with flat rock, and building a fire. When the rocks were red hot, they would rake out the embers, then line the stones with ferns, bush branches or other vegetation. They would put in up to one hundred pounds of bulbs at a time, then cover them with branches, soil and mats. They made a hole with a stick, poured water in and allowed the bulbs to steam for a day or so. When they were cooked, they would strip the bark and press the bulbs flat like pancakes. They smell like vanilla and taste like brown or maple sugar. They were also used to sweeten other foods in the days before sugar. Blue camas bulbs can be made into a molasses by boiling them until the water is almost evaporated. Many early white settlers learned of blue camas from Native people and used this bulb to spice up an otherwise monotonous diet.

Although blue camas appears starchy, it does not contain starch. It contains inulin, a complex sugar also found in dandelion root and Jerusalem artichoke. Because of inulin, which effects the action of the pancreas, blue camas was eaten regularly by Native people to help keep the blood sugar level in balance and avoid diabetes. If eaten excessively, blue camas can act as a purgative and emetic.

What a marvelous plant for Beaver people who, like it, can be conscious of beauty and practicality at the same time. In flower, camas inspires those who see it with its beauty. Abloom in a wide meadow, it looks like a blue lake. Up close its delicate flowers fascinate you with their beauty and their precision. Even the white death camas is beautiful to behold. Yet the blue camas, besides giving joy, also gives a food that was used to sustain people for thousands of years. Blue camas was one of the gifts of the Earth Mother that gave stability of diet and health to Native people.

Like their plant, Beaver people have the ability to sustain those with whom they are associated. Because their own roots go deeply into the earth, they are able to give a firm footing to people or projects with which they are associated. Like the blue camas bulb, they can both sustain and sweeten things with which they are involved, for their stability is usually sweetened by the contentment they are capable of feeling and transmitting when they are in balance with the energies coming through them.

As the good qualities of blue camas are reversed in death camas, so the good qualities of Beaver people can be reversed when their energies are not allowed to flow smoothly through them. During these periods Beaver people can become so crystallized in their stability that they can literally choke the life out of themselves and any things that they touch. When Beaver people do not feel contentment, they transmit this disharmony as greatly as they otherwise transmit harmony. At these times Beaver people could use the mental equivalent of an excessive amount of blue camas to get them moving again, at least in some way.

The color of Beaver people is blue, the brilliant blue of the camas flower or of the pure blue chrysocolla. For them this blue signifies physical tranquillity and psychological contentment stemming from a feeling of peace and happiness. These feelings that come from the color blue are necessary for Beaver people to have before they can work with the spiritual aspects of this color. Beaver people must be happily grounded on the earth plane before they can discover the spiritual aspirations that are also within them.

Being born under the Frogs Return Moon, the second moon of Wabun to the East, gives Beaver people a gentle prod toward constantly growing, since this is one of the spring moons during which all things on the earth begin to stir and grow. This impetus is necessary so that Beaver folks will not get caught too rigidly in their own ideas of contentment coming only from complete stability. Being under the direction of Wabun also encourages these folks to go beyond the material level and seek whatever spiritual illumination they can find.

As mentioned previously, their membership in the Turtle clan increases the rootedness and stability of Beaver people and intensifies many of their other traits. Being from this clan means that they have to firmly guard against becoming too stubborn or unmoving in any of their thoughts, feelings or actions, or they can very effectively block the flow of life's energy which sustains them.

The beaver, the animal totem of those born under the Frogs Return Moon, is, outside of man, the only animal capable of changing its environment drastically in order to provide for its own peace, security and contentment. The beaver is the largest rodent in this country, the second largest in the world, after the South American capybara. Adult beavers can weigh between thirty and seventy pounds, and they never stop growing. A beaver can be as much as three to four feet long. It has a body amazingly engineered to suit its habits and habitat. While it is a land mammal, it spends a lot of time in the water. Its lungs and cardiovascular system are designed to allow it to store enough oxygen to remain underwater for fifteen minutes or more.

It has a large, broad, flat, scaly tail, which serves as a rudder when it is swimming and a balancer when it is working on land. Its front paws are very nimble, allowing it to hold and turn a branch it is eating much as we hold corn on the cob, and to enable it to carry mud and leaves necessary for its construction work. Its rear paws are webbed and as large as a Ping-Pong paddle when extended, giving it its amazing swimming speed and ability. Its brown fur is dense and is kept waterproof by the oil that its musk gland secretes. Its teeth are large, high crowned and capable of repairing or replacing themselves if they are hurt or lost, a most necessary thing for an animal that cuts down many trees both for eating and for building. Beavers have folds of skin behind their incisors which seal their mouth, allowing them to work underwater without drowning. They have valvelike ears and nostrils which automatically close when they are underwater, and clear membranes which shield their eyes.

With such magnificently adapted bodies you would expect to find beavers all over the place, especially since they have few natural predators and amazing defenses against them. We might have them all over now if it weren't for the fact that beavers have two things that men felt they needed more than the beavers: their fur, long used for making gentlemen's hats, and their musk gland, which secretes castoreum, regarded as a cure-all at least from the time of the early Greeks until the eighteenth century. Castoreum contains salicylic acid, one of the main ingredients in aspirin, and was and still is used as a fixative in expensive perfumes. Beaver was in such demand that the search for them probably did as much to motivate white exploration of this continent as anything else. From the 1600s the Hudson's Bay Company sent trappers in large numbers to get beavers, and many fortunes, including that of the Astors, were built upon beaver pelts. Because of their value to humans, beavers were almost driven to extinction by the 1800s. Even as late as 1907 to 1909 the average annual catch of beavers here was about eighty thousand. By 1912 it dropped to seventeen thousand, luckily for both us and the beavers.

Beavers, humans finally discovered, helped the water table and were of great value to fishing, wildlife, vegetation and aesthetics. This help comes about because of the dams and lodges most beavers build to protect themselves and keep comfortable. These amazing log constructions, shored up by mud and leaves, help to maintain old ponds and create new ones where other plants and animals can live. Beavers' dams and canals are the work of natural engineers. Canals, which can extend seven hundred feet or more, are usually built on a number of levels with locks at intervals to maintain a proper water level. Beavers use them to maintain water deep enough to float a log into their pond so they can have sufficient food and repair materials for their dams. The dams are built so the beaver will have a deep body of water, of a fairly constant level, year round. A beaver needs its pond to remain safe from predators and to keep enough food to last throughout the winter, when it is more difficult to get trees, the staple of the beaver's diet. They eat the leaves and the sweet inner bark and use the logs for construction. Their favorite is quaking aspen bark, a fact that Otter people should note.

Beavers don't talk much. There is an occasional bark, hiss or squeal, but they usually make a soft mew, and this only in their lodge. They slap the water with their tails as a warning of danger. Beavers mate for life, and usually live in colonies of about five. They are affectionate parents who keep their children around for two years, or until the next litter of kits comes. At this time, they run them off, and they must look for their own mate and lodge. When the babies are born, the mother runs the father off until the kits are able to get around. He spends his exile with other husbands who have also been asked to leave. Old males who lose their mates sometimes become surly, and some people say the beavers in the colony then hold a council to decide whether or not to drive the disharmonious one off. Such old beavers usually live alone in a bank den, not even bothering to find a lodge.

People of this totem, like the beaver, are capable of drastically altering their environments in order to provide for their own peace, security and contentment. They can, and will, make alterations on any number of levels: physical, mental or emotional. Like the beaver, they will make these alterations in a slow, deliberate but constant and resourceful way. Once they have their environment in order, they will, like their totem, make repairs whenever necessary to make sure that it remains that way. An orderly, secure setting is really necessary for Beaver people to work and grow, and it must be orderly on all of the levels previously mentioned. It is not that Beaver people can't change, it is just that they can grow more easily when they have a setting that gives them a feeling of security and contentment.

Like the beaver, most people of this totem have some attraction to the water: to swimming or sailing, or just walking around lakes, rivers or ponds. The water seems to allow them to see things more clearly and put their lives in better perspective. Beaver people are clever and nimble. They are quick to learn anything that they feel is necessary or beneficial for them to know.

Like the beaver, they also have bodies and minds that quickly adapt themselves to their environment, once they have set the environment in order. Because of this, these folks can be successful in any field or endeavor to which they apply themselves. They are patient and persevering people and will usually obtain whatever they set their minds to because of these qualities. They are also creative people, especially on the physical level. You will rarely see a Beaver person's lodge that will not show a great deal of originality in its decor. They will spend a lot of time and creativity on designing just the right backdrop for their own personalities. This creative energy can be put to other uses with as amazing results.

Beaver people, like their totem, have minds capable of wonderful feats of engineering, whether they put their minds on their homes, their jobs or their friends. When they determine that things need changing to function better, things will change. Given some time, Beaver people can redesign most jobs or work projects to run better, smoother and more harmoniously for all of the people involved. They will sometimes put this creative energy to work to help their friends and loved ones redesign their lives to work in a more content and tranquil way. When they have done all this, they will turn their energies toward the spiritual realms in which they can also be at home.

These folks often don't talk too much, when they are not certain of their surroundings or the people in them. Once they get to know people, however, they will express their thoughts quite readily. Their feelings are another thing. These they can hold back as effectively as the beaver's dam holds back the water. Beaver people must learn to let their feelings out a little at a time, or they run the risk of someday being drowned in a flash flood of emotion. It is a difficult task for them to learn to do this, as they are self-reliant people and usually feel that they should not burden others with their own problems.

If Beaver people don't learn to express more feelings and to accept life with its changes, they can become very stubborn and unhappy, and will, in this condition, often overindulge themselves in food, drink or anything else that will dull their feeling of discontent. If they continue long in this state, blocking themselves from what they need, they can develop blockages in their neck or throat or can damage their liver or gallbladder through overindulgence.

Beaver people, like their totem, take relationships very seriously. When they find a mate, they sincerely hope it will be for life. The stability of a good relationship often gives them the contentment they need to grow in other directions and they will lavish affection upon those whom they love. These folks make good parents, like the Beaver. Females will tend to be very devoted, almost territorial, about their children, especially when very young. They also can make the mistake of doing the same thing the beaver female does and driving off the male by ignoring him and giving all of her attention to the child. As the children get older, Beaver people will loosen the ropes on them, and they often will make a real push to get their children out of the lodge, when it is the right time for them to make their own lives. They have a good sense of timing on this.

As children, Beaver people can be testy until they have an established routine. Once they have that, they will be contented children and usually quite well behaved. They are creative and can easily amuse themselves for long periods of time. However, Beaver children are not the kind to take on long trips with vague destinations. The insecurities that this kind of traveling gives them will dampen the fun of anyone involved.

Beaver people complement those of the Snake clan. They are most easily compatible with their fellow members of the Turtle clan, those of the Snow Goose and the Brown Bear, and with those of the Frog clan, Cougar and Flicker people.

As people from other totems travel through this place on the wheel, they can learn how to set their own houses in order on this earth plane, so that, whatever they seek, they can seek it from a place of tranquillity and contentment. They can also learn the value of stability, of patience and perseverance, and they can learn better how to root themselves in the Earth Mother who sustains us all.

Cornplanting Moon (Deer)
May 21–June 20

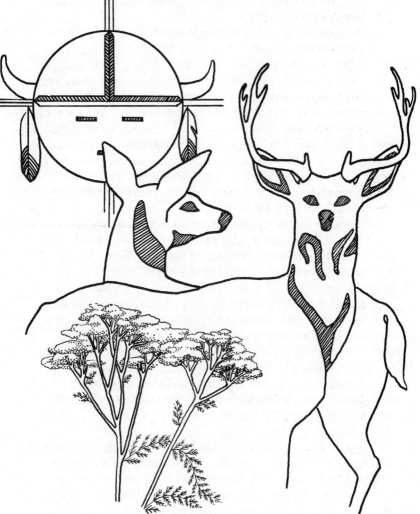

People born under the Cornplanting Moon, which falls between May 21 and June 20, have the moss agate as their totem in the mineral kingdom, the yarrow as their totem in the plant kingdom and the deer as their totem in the animal kingdom. Their colors are white and green, and they are of the Butterfly elemental clan.

Their stone, the moss agate, is a fibrous form of chalcedony, or cryptocrystalline quartz. In all agates the colors of the stone are distributed either haphazardly or in curved bands. In the case of moss agate, the bands of color are distributed in such a way that the stone looks as though it contains preserved moss. Until this century people believed that the patterns were caused by moss. Scientific analysis showed the "moss" to be manganese oxide, iron or other minerals. The most common form of moss agate now is translucent white quartz with green moss within or whitish or bluish quartz with black moss. Moss agates are found in most parts of the country and in other places in the world. They are most commonly found in the beds of streams or rivers.

The moss agate is a healing stone. It used to be considered most beneficial for the eyes, but it has also been used, in pendulum style, to heal other parts of the body. Some people have carried moss agate in their pockets or on their persons in order to experience its healing properties. Since the stone appears to contain delicate vegetation, it has been considered to be a link between the mineral and plant kingdoms, enabling its owner to have a better understanding of both of these. The ancient peoples believed that keeping moss agate pebbles in the mouth would allay thirst. They also felt that, because of the stone's ability to connect the mineral and plant kingdom, it had particular powers for helping rain to come when the plants were in need of it. For this reason, they used the stone in some of their ceremonies to invite rain.

Like their stone, Deer people have particular healing abilities, if they learn to develop them. People in this totem can have abilities in almost any field if they are willing to work at getting them. These folks, like the moss agate, are beneficial to the eyes of those around them. Deer people like beauty, and they like to make their environments beautiful. They are often capable of creating things of beauty out of very ordinary materials. With these abilities, homes, offices or other places that Deer people go will become more attractive places to be for anyone involved with them.

People of this totem, like their stone, have special abilities to link up their minds with their relations in the mineral and plant kingdoms. They are usually attracted strongly to both plants and minerals, and they have the talent for bringing representatives of these two kingdoms together in many attractive ways, whether in a terrarium or in a garden. People of the Deer are most comfortable when they can spend at least part of their time in the mountainous or hilly country where the Earth Mother has joined together the other elements with which they feel a special closeness.

Yarrow, the plant totem for the people of the Deer, is a beautiful, useful and versatile plant. It is very prolific. Yarrow can be found in almost any exposed area, be it in the city or the country. It has a strong scent and a sharp, astringent taste, due to the tannic and achilleine acid it contains. It is a perennial, with leaves that are finely divided into numerous narrow divisions making it almost look like a fuzzy fern on a stem. Its leaves are one of the first ones out during the spring, and, by summer, it can grow to three feet tall. Its white flowers bloom most of the summer. They grow on top of the stalk in small, numerous heads which form a flat-topped arrangement. The flowers can measure up to one foot across. Yarrow, in the European tradition, is called *Achillea millefolium,* after Achilles, of Greek history, who is credited with discovering the medicinal values of the plant, though it is likely people in this country knew of them quite some time before. The Ojibwa people called yarrow *wabeno-wusk,* herb of the dawn or herb of the East Wind.

The whole plant can be used medicinally. Native people here used it as a tonic for those who were run-down or had problems with their digestive tract. Yarrow will keep up your strength while cleansing your blood, opening up your pores to allow for elimination of toxins through the skin, and soothing your mucous membranes. Because of these qualities, yarrow is very useful for colds, flu and related diseases. Taken when you first get a cold, yarrow can sometimes rid you of it within twenty-four hours.

Yarrow will also work as a diuretic, if you are in need of one, but it will not have this effect if you are not. It is also useful during pregnancy and at birth to prevent hemorrhage. Externally, yarrow acts as a local anesthetic and disinfectant. If you chew a leaf and put it on a mosquito bite, it will soon relieve the itch and discomfort. It is purported to help to relieve toothaches when chewed. Achilles said that the juice put in the eye will relieve redness. People from the Orient use the stalks of the yarrow when they cast their I Ching.

The yarrow can be useful to people of the Deer, as they are often prone to diseases of the lungs, glands and bronchial tubes. While Deer people are in good balance, these diseases will usually not be more serious than colds or flus that strike them in their respiratory system. Yarrow is excellent in helping to cure these. Externally, yarrow is also good for them in helping to anesthetize and disinfect the bumps and scratches they sometimes get when they lose control of their energy and jump too quickly, often bumping their bodies into things that hurt.

How much like Deer people their herb is! They, too, are useful and versatile people, concerned with bringing beauty to the world that they inhabit. They can be found all over the place, in just about any exposed area, doing any variety of work or play. Like yarrow, they are easy to spot because of their versatility. Deer folks, like their plant, can be astringent. They sometimes have a cutting edge to their humor, especially if they feel themselves cornered in any way or if they have ventured into a field with which they are not quite comfortable. While their outsides seem made of honey, they are quite capable of having a stream of vinegar running through them.

Deer people, like yarrow, are a tonic to those around them. Usually, their energy is so high that it can float a couple of other people along in its wake. Deer people make good friends who will help you to keep up your strength through any problems that you encounter. They will encourage you to open yourself up to them and to life and to let out anything that is bothering you. As long as you do so in an interesting way, they will be more than happy to listen to all you have to say. But don't get repetitious with your Deer friends. Their minds race around too fast to allow them the natural patience to listen to the same problems over and over again. When you finish, sometimes before, they will start to soothe you with their real concern and various charms. Deer folks really like people, and they will sincerely try to make any of their friends feel better, no matter what the problem. They do get a little nervous, though, if you get into any area that they consider too personal or too deep. They feel that if they listen to you open up in such an honest way, you will expect them to do the same. And Deer people, for all their gregariousness, are very slow to open the depths of their beings to any other person.

Deer people do have the gift of gab. The like to talk about any subject, with anyone, unless the subject is too personal, at which time they will change the topic of conversation so easily and charmingly that you won't even notice they forgot to answer that question about themselves and their lives.

Like yarrow and their stone, the moss agate, Deer people can be healers fairly easily. Like both of these totems, they have a special gift for helping to clear up and heal the eyes of people they work with, enabling them to see things more clearly. Yet they frequently don't have the ability to see clearly themselves because their eye is so busy roving from one idea to another that they don't take the time to really know the truth of any one thing.

Being of the Butterfly clan increases this tendency of Deer people to jump quickly from one thing to another. All Butterfly people tend to spend a lot of time fluttering through the air, examining one thing after another and never really being quite ready to settle into anything. However, the moon of Deer people, the Cornplanting Moon, being the last moon of spring when things have settled into their pattern of growth, does help to bring them a bit of stability and imparts to them some of the wisdom of Wabun, the Spirit Keeper of the East. At this time during the season of Wabun the seeds are in the ground, have germinated and begun to take on their proper shape and form. Wabun's gift of illlumination comes to Deer people most easily when they have learned what their proper shape and form are.

The colors of the Deer people are white and green. Their white is the translucent white of formlessness, of the space where anything seems to be possible. It is the white of a child coming into the world in perfect purity and innocence. As this white contains within itself all of the other colors, Deer people tend to contain myriad possibilities in themselves. Their green is the green of nature, of healing and restoring. However, their green can turn into a color of self-righteousness, of a person who wants his own opinions always to prevail.

The animal totem of those born during the Cornplanting Moon is, of course, the deer, that sensitive, graceful and alert creature who brings beauty and joy to all who see him. In this country we have three main species of deer: the mule deer, the white-tailed deer and the black-tailed deer. Each tends to inhabit a separate area, with the mule deer living in all western states and Canada; the whitetail mainly living in the East, although some, mainly transplants from eastern herds, are in California and the Northwest; and the blacktail living in the Cascades and the Sierra Nevada. All of these deer are fairly adaptable, although the blacktail has a decided preference for forested areas.

While there are some differences in sizes and habits of these three types, they all tend to range between two and four feet at the shoulder and between fifty and four hundred pounds. The whitetail is the smallest, and the mule is usually the largest. The whitetail is named that because it has a tail white on the underside, which it raises and uses to flash signals to its compatriots. The blacktail has a black tail, and the mule deer has large ears, which look almost like those of a mule. Deer have a bleating voice, sometimes resembling that of a sheep. They snort when excited, squeal when under attack or in pain, and do sometimes have a special bleat with which to call their fawns. Black-tailed and white-tailed deer move in a series of graceful bounds, while the mule deer has a kind of stiff-legged jump. The basic body color of the white-tailed deer and mule deer is reddish brown in summer, becoming gray in winter. Black-tailed deer are dark brown or dark gray, with white underparts. The fawns of all deer are spotted when they are born, as a measure to protect them while they lie in camouflage for the first six to eight weeks of life, until they are able to run with their mothers. Fawns are born without a scent, in order to afford them further protection.

Bucks have sets of antlers which they lose every year and then regrow. It is said that they lose them to keep them weak while the fawns are young so they will not bother the does or fawns. They lose their antlers in January or February and don't have a full set back until the mating season in late fall. While the

Strong Sun Moon (Flicker)
June 21–July 22

antlers are growing and are in the soft, velvet stage, the bucks have to be careful, as the growing antlers are full of blood and very delicate. The growth process saps some of their physical vitality.

Deer live in herds, or small groups with others of their own sex, except for the mating season. During this time bucks are very single-minded in their activities. Unlike other members of the deer family, they don't try to attract a harem. They bound from doe to doe, depending on the interest of the females. During this season bucks who have been great friends during the early part of the year often enter into combat with their now fully grown antlers. Usually the combat is not fatal, unless the horns get locked and the bucks starve. After mating, deer herds are usually led for the winter by an older doe. In the spring the does give birth, often to twins or even triplets. These multiple births sometimes cause overpopulation, and then in lean winters, when the leaves, shoots, buds, roots and grass are scarce, many deer die of starvation. Their predators are cougars, coyotes, dogs, bears, bobcats, forest fires, humans and automobiles. It is estimated that over 400,000 deer are killed annually on highways and other roads.

Like their totem, Deer people are sensitive, graceful, fast-moving and alert. They are by nature intuitive, and this helps them to sense easily the feelings of other people, at least those on the surface. Since their own feelings move so quickly, they have usually experienced most of the moods that others can be in. This helps to give them their ability to listen, even if only with one ear, and still understand what their friends and associates are feeling. They frequently find it difficult to listen fully to others because their own thoughts and feelings are sparked by what the other person is saying. Their own thoughts begin to move by them so quickly that they feel they just have to express them before they get away completely. Yet Deer people are usually so graceful in the way they bring their own feelings into the conversation that you often don't even realize you are being interrupted. Because of their alertness, Deer people will sense when they are interrupting too much and will stop and listen more closely, so that you don't ever go away with the feeling that you haven't been given their best attention.

The need for beauty around them really runs deep within Deer people. They like to be surrounded by beautiful scenery or homes and by people that they sense are beautiful on some if not all levels. This does not mean that they will only have physically beautiful people around them. These folks are intuitive and sensitive enough to know that beauty can be within as well as without. And, like the deer, these people do often bring joy to those who know them. They want to be able to do this for others, since they understand that joy is necessary in order for people to appreciate the beauty of the world.

Deer people are clever, resourceful and creative. They know how to make something beautiful out of the most simple materials, both on a physical and an emotional level. They are often artists in some medium, or musicians, and this art brings a real sense of fulfillment to their souls. Sometimes this will be manifested in unique ways. Perhaps they will create culinary works of art, perfect herbal tinctures or magnificently conceived theories, rather than oil paintings or watercolors. The medium doesn't matter to them as long as they can create and as long as the result is something of beauty. Emotionally, Deer people are able to draw the beauty out of those around them, by their true concern, their sensitivity, and their cleverness. They really see the beauty in other people, and they always try to find ways to reflect this to the other.

Like the Deer, these folks have a wide range of sounds they make, and they usually voice themselves in an enthusiastic way. This enthusiasm is contagious. When a Deer person starts laughing, often everyone in the room is in stitches.

Sometimes Deer people share another trait with their totem that does not always have positive results for them. Because they like so many people so much, they often find it difficult to settle in one relationship. There are so many people they find truly attractive that it is sometimes almost impossible for them to choose just one. This is true of both men and women of this totem, although it is often more pronounced in the male. Like the deer, these folks also enjoy being with people of their own gender, sharing the special qualities that they have in common with them.

Deer people have lessons that they must learn about being able to find a relationship in which they can be comfortable enough to open up the parts of their beings that they usually try to hide from others. They also need to learn to value some consistency in their life, or they can spend all of their time jumping from one idea to another, without ever really accomplishing what they want to. They find it difficult to balance their time and their energies and to organize their lives in an effective manner. If they don't learn how to do these things, they can make themselves prone to diseases that will slow them down forcibly or to conditions in which their bodies become as jumpy and nervous as their minds can be. If they don't learn to find people to whom they can open, they may also become prone to blockages in their systems.

Deer people make loving parents, although they sometimes have quite an adjustment in matching their pace to that of a child. Like does, Deer people may want to leave their babies in a safe camouflage while they go about the business of their life, coming back only when it is time for nurturing and loving them. Deer men have more of a problem with parenthood than do the women. It just seems foreign to them and they have to mak a real effort to involve themselves with the process of a baby's growth. When the child is older and able to run with the parent both are happier with the situation.

Deer children, being sensitive and intuitive, as well as creat are usually able to amuse themselves a good part of the time They also like to amuse others and give them joy, much as o Deer people do. Like fawns, they can easily blend with the surroundings and keep themselves quiet so that no harm cc to them from any quarter. Since they are often quiet, eas amused and amusing, Deer children make the model chilc that all parents wish they had had.

While people of this totem find it easy to get along with other people, they are particularly compatible with Raven Otter people, their Butterfly clan relations, and with Red H Sturgeon people, of the Thunderbird clan. Their comple the other of the Thunderbird clan, Elk people.

When people of other moons find themselves in this they will discover something of their own abilities to be sensitive, fast-moving and appreciative of beauty in all forms. They will also discover the strengths and weakn come from having life's energy run through them so q

Those born under the Strong Sun Moon, between June 21 and July 22, have the carnelian agate as their totem in the mineral kingdom, the wild rose as their totem in the plant kingdom and the flicker as their totem in the animal kingdom. Their color is the pink of the rose and the flicker, and they are of the Frog elemental clan.

Their mineral, like the moss agate, is a chalcedony, a crypto-crystalline variety of quartz. Carnelian is a clear chalcedony, which ranges in color from pink to red to yellow. The yellow variety is usually referred to as sard. In proper usage the term "carnelian" is only applied to translucent stone. The opaque form of these stones is jasper.

Carnelian has been widely used from early times for jewelry and other ornaments. It may be the first hard stone that was engraved in ancient times. Because of its color, the carnelian has been associated with blood. It was considered to be an emergency stone useful in healing people who had been accidentally injured and was said to have the property of stopping the flow of blood from wounds. In emergencies it was suspended from a string or thong and used, pendulum style, over the wound. Its circular movement was believed to stop bleeding and start the healing process.

Because of its color and properties, carnelian is also associated with the heart. A gift of carnelian was a gift of the heart, and so the stone was often given to represent a pledge of love. In older times people believed that carrying the carnelian would help to keep the heart healthy and open to all the emotions that center in it. Mothers would often carry carnelian to make sure that their hearts remained open to the needs of their children.

Like their stone, people of the Flicker are often associated with the idea of ornamentation, especially of the home, because having a comfortable and beautiful dwelling is very important to them. Flicker people are very home-oriented, and they function best when their home, be it physical, mental or emotional, is in proper order and an attractive place to be. Like their stone, Flicker people are easily engraved with new thoughts and feelings, and once this engraving has been done, they are very solid in their belief in whatever new concepts have been put upon them. However, before they allow any new things to come into their lives, they will take quite some time to analyze and weigh what they are and how they will fit with the other concepts that govern their lives.

Flicker people, like carnelian, are associated with the blood, both literally and figuratively. People of this totem have a special connection with the spleen, the blood reservoir of the body, as well as with the breast and stomach. They have the ability to flow freely with life, much as the blood flows freely through a healthy body. Flicker people, like their stone, are useful to have around in an emergency, as their intuitive powers can help them to see what the nature of the emergency really is, and their concern can help the injured person to feel that they are being cared for in the best possible way.

Flicker folks are people who are really sensitive to their own hearts and the messages that it can give to them. If a Flicker person decides that he or she loves you, this is a love that you can count upon being solid and stable, short of treachery on your part. When they are in good balance, people of this totem are very open to their fellow humans and very loving. Their hearts are capable of overflowing with love for all those around them, in the mineral, plant and animal as well as human kingdoms. Flicker people usually make very loving parents, willing to sacrifice much for the happiness of their children, and they often have a very open definition of who their children are. They are the folks who will often have a house full of children, their own mixed in with all of the other kids in the neighborhood who feel the need for a little extra love and attention. And Flicker folks will give this love abundantly.

The plant for people of this totem is the wild rose, that beautiful bush that has inspired reams of poetry and untold stanzas of song. The wild rose is an erect shrub with thorny stems and compound leaves that have five- to seven-toothed leaflets. They are similar to domesticated rose leaves but smaller. The flowers have five petals arranged around a large yellow center. They can range from pale to bright pink. After the flowers disappear, the roses begin to form their fruit, called hips, which are orange and look like berries. Many hips have a fleshy outer rind and small white seeds in the center; but others are seedless.

While many herbalists classify the rind as being bland tasting, others feel it has a subtle spicy, quite distinct flavor. Rose hips are one of the richest sources of vitamin C. The roses bloom from May until July, deliciously scenting all of the land around them, and then the hips are ready to harvest in the fall.

You can eat the hips raw all fall and winter, as the Native people did in the areas where wild roses grew, or you can dry them, make them into tea, grind them for meal or flour, or use them in jam or soups. It is said that boiling them extracts about 40 percent of the vitamin C, and drying extracts about 65 percent. You can find recipes in older cookbooks if they aren't available in your modern ones.

Rose hips, because of their vitamin C content, are excellent remedies for colds, sore throats and flu. Rose petals, steeped in boiling water, make a delicate tea which is said to have a slight astringent and tonic effect on the body. The twigs and roots can also be peeled and boiled to make tea, and this is reputed to be helpful for colds. Years ago rose hip tea was used to dissolve and remove gallstones and kidney stones and to cleanse the bloodstream of people who had blood or liver problems. At those times the distilled water of the leaves and flowers was also used to strengthen the heart, refresh the spirits and help with problems of the body that required a gentle cooling effect.

Native people used rose hips, along with mint and raspberry, to make a tea for children as well as adults that helped to keep them happy and healthy. According to a Mohawk herbalist, there is an Indian prophecy that says that after the Europeans came to this continent there would be a great need for a cure for malignancies that would otherwise cause the downfall of their civilization. This cure for cancer would come, says the prophecy, from a hybrid rose developed by a person of Indian descent.

Rose water, made from the flowers, was frequently used in older times in eye lotions and to give relief from eye discomfort caused by hay fever. The rose was also used by herbalists to cover the smell of less pleasantly scented herbs that had to be ingested. Rose petals are made into an oil which is used for a perfume or hair rinse, and the dried petals are one of the main components of sachets, used to scent clothes, drawers and closets.

From their plant, Flicker people can learn of the wide variety of abilities that are available to them when they are properly flowing with the energy of life. Like the rose, they can be truly beautiful people, capable of inspiring others with both their beauty and their usefulness. Flicker people, like their plant, have a wild quality about them and a special attractiveness when they are in a natural setting. When their lives are in flower, they bring happiness to all who behold them, and when the flowers of one stage wither, they are replaced with the hips of the wisdom that that stage has produced. Like the rose hip, Flicker people are most often sought out for their outer rinds, the visible attributes that they abundantly have, whether physical or emotional. Yet, inside of these people are deeper knowledges that are just as useful as the visible ones, if people take the time to dig through to them.

Flicker people who are not in balance may appear bland like some say the rose hip is. In this state they can even be slothful and more involved in undeveloped emotions than in anything more real and lasting. When out of balance, Flicker folks seem like they are not capable of independent thought and action and stable emotional relationships. However, when they are balanced, Flicker people are extremely sensitive and able both to absorb and to reflect the things that are around them. They are quite capable of making a decision, whether of the mind or emotions, and of sticking to it.

Rose hip or rose petal tea can be useful to people of this totem to keep their blood in a clean and pure state and to help with any colds or flu so that these disorders will not spread and attack the stomach, liver or other sensitive internal organs. These teas can also help to strengthen the hearts of Flicker people, as their sometimes indiscriminate outpouring of love can leave them feeling weak. The well-balanced Flicker person will usually be in very good health and can just enjoy the flowers and fruit of their plant as a tasty, delightfully scented beverage that can help keep them happy and healthy.

The color of Flicker people is pink, which can either be the pink of immaturity or of universal, all-healing love, depending upon the individual growth of the person involved. Flicker people who have not yet found their balance will often find themselves consumed by the raging sea of their own emotions, and this will keep them from coming to a place of harmony and balance. However, those who have found their direction in life will be able to channel their own emotions and sensitivity in such a way that it will help all those that they touch.

The shifting emotional nature of the Flicker people is, of course, intensified because they are of the Frog clan. Members of this clan often find themselves carried along by the force of their own feelings, flowing strongly but in no set direction.

As the first of the peoples governed by Shawnodese, Spirit Keeper of the South, Flicker folks have their natural inclinations strengthened even more because Shawnodese governs the time of rapid growth and the quality of trust. This pushes Flicker people to experience their emotions even more intensely so that they have the ability to grow in their lives as much as they can and to grow with trust.

Their moon, that of the Strong Sun, does give them some stability and slows them down a bit, as the time of the strong sun is the season when we must grow quickly, but only in the proper direction, as the sun saps our strength for tangential activities at the same time it helps us to grow in our proper course. This is the moon of the summer solstice, the time when all things of the earth must begin their journey toward flowering and bearing fruit.

The animal totem for those born during the Strong Sun Moon is the flicker, that most numerous and mystical member of the woodpecker family. The American name for the woodpecker is derived from that of the Latin god Picus, with whom Circe fell in love. When she asked him to accept the sun as a father-in-law, he refused and was turned into a woodpecker. There are two kinds of flickers in the United States. The yellow-shafted flicker, named because of his yellow underwings, is usually found east of the Great Plains, while the red-shafted flicker, named because of his red, almost coral, underwings, lives west of the Great Plains. Both flickers are grayish brown, with a white rump, red crescent on nape, black crescent on breast and black spots below. Both types of flickers are found in a variety of places: woods, farms and even suburbs. Unlike other woodpeckers, they spend quite a bit of time on the ground and will perch upright on limbs as songbirds do. They are drummers, playing their song on dead limbs, tin roofs and wooden houses, sometimes to extract insects and sometimes for the sheer joy of playing. During mating they put on an especially magnificent display of their musical talents.

Flickers eat insects and wild seeds and berries, with an occasional addition of grain or corn. They have several varieties of song. One sounds like *yuk-yuk-yuk;* another, *wicker-wicker-wicker;* another, "wake up, wake up," sometimes interpreted "cheer up, cheer up"; yet another is *cook-cook-cook-cook.* The flicker's flight is strong and direct, once it takes off with a series of wavelike leaps upward and downward. Like other woodpeckers, the flicker has a stout, sharp bill, a long tongue and two toes in front and two behind with sharp, curved claws to allow it to cling to trees while it digs for larvae.

The flicker digs a gourd-shaped hole in a tree trunk for its nest, and this is often used later by other birds. These nests are usually eight to twenty-five feet high, and the openings to them are two inches in diameter. Flickers can have from six to twenty-five eggs, with eight being the median number. Like most birds, flickers are good and caring parents, taking proper care of their young until it is time to cast them out of the nest and allow them to fly on their own.

The flicker is a special bird to many of the Native people in this country. He is considered to be a courageous bird. Legend says he has red wings because he went too close to a fire set by the Earthquake Spirit to try to put it out, and the flames from it colored his wings and tail red. Flickers are especially valued because of their drumming. Their drumbeat, like the beat of any drum, represents the beat of the heart and the beat of the earth. Because of their song, they are considered special birds, and their feathers are used in many religious articles and ceremonies. Because their feathers are red, they are associated with blood and are often presented to war spirits. Red feathers on prayer sticks are considered war offerings, against either human or spiritual enemies. Flicker feathers worn in the hair designate the wearer as a member of a medicine society.

From the Flicker, folks of this moon can learn of their latent mystical talents, which only come out when they are balanced in very harmonious surroundings. Flicker people do have the ability to pierce through this level of reality and see things in different ways. Because of this, they are very intuitive, and the perceptions that come to them in this manner are the things that most help them to decide upon their proper direction in life. Many Flicker folks don't realize what guides them and find it difficult to explain to others how they make their decisions. More logical people often feel that Flicker folks are sloppy, irrational thinkers because they heavily rely on their intuitions without even realizing what they are doing.

Like their totem, people of this moon need to be able to drum and sing their song in life, whatever they perceive that song to be. But, before they feel balanced enough to do that singing, they must first have a comfortable nest. Home is very important to Flicker people. More than most people they have a true love of home, and they are not happy when they don't have a comfortable and harmonious homeplace to return to after any flights that they take. Part of that harmonious home must be people with whom they feel a true oneness. Flicker people, like their bird, make good nests to be used by them and by others. No matter how beautiful their dwelling, they do not feel it is complete if it is not shared by others they really love. Relationship is very important to these folks, and they will give much of their energy to establishing and maintaining good relationships with others.

Like the Flicker, folks with this totem are good parents, ones who give their children lavish amounts of love and deep feelings of security. Unlike the bird, they sometimes have a difficult time letting their little ones go when it is time for them to leave the nest. Being able to show their love in this way is one of the hardest tests for Flicker people to pass.

Flicker children tend to be somewhat demanding. They need to be given as much love as they will give in turn when they mature. They need frequent reassurances that they are loved, and they have a strong need for a secure homelife. In return, they will give those around them all of the love and attention they are capable of summoning. If they receive what they need when they are young, it is much easier for them to reach a good balance as they grow older.

Once Flicker people of any age have happy and secure homes, they will turn their nurturing instincts to larger targets. Flicker folks will love their extended family, then everyone in their neighborhood, then their country. But this loving fraternity is not enough, as they are sufficiently intuitive to know that their love cannot be absorbed by large and arbitrary groups. This is the point at which it is essential for Flicker people to go within to hear the songs of their own hearts and learn who the proper targets for their love and devotion should be.

Usually they will find groups with which they can harmonize, and they will learn to sing their song in the chorus that is the proper one for them. This could be a charitable or fraternal organization, but will more frequently be one with more religious or mystical leanings, as the mystical nature of Flicker people needs to be fulfilled once they have found material security and well-being. Once Flicker people find a group that shares their direction, they will be very devoted to it and they will usually find great happiness at being able to channel all the loving energy that can flow through them. Flicker people do need something to serve that is larger than themselves or their families.

If they cannot find the material peace that enables them to continue their quest, they will often be very unhappy people, spending most of their time wallowing in the negative emotions that can flow through them. During such periods they will be prone to a variety of internal disorders that stem from energy and blood not flowing in their correct channels. At such times Flicker people need to find reassurance on both the material and spiritual levels in order to effect a total cure.

When people from other totems find themselves in this place on the Medicine Wheel, they will be able to learn about their own needs for giving and receiving love and for following their own perceptions and intuitions. They will also learn about their own sense of security and their personal need to find a spiritual direction that helps them to channel the life energy that always flows through all of us.

Flicker people are compatible with their fellow members of the Frog clan, those of the Cougar and the Snake, and with those of the Turtle clan, the Brown Bear, Beaver and Snow Goose people. They especially complement those of the Snow Goose.

Ripe Berries Moon (Sturgeon)
July 23–August 22

People born from July 23 until August 22 are born during the Ripe Berries Moon. Their mineral totem is the garnet and iron, their plant totem is the raspberry and their animal totem is the sturgeon. Their color is red, and they belong to the Thunderbird elemental clan.

Their gemstone, the garnet, is a silicate crystal, which is fairly hard, with a resinous luster. There are six types of garnet minerals which run from red to brown, green, yellow, black and white. The four aluminum silicates that form garnets are almandine, which is deep red or violet red; grossularite, which is golden yellow or reddish yellow; pyrope, which runs deep red to black; and spessartite, which is red or, more often, brown. The iron garnet is andradite, which can be wine to yellow or green or black. The chromium garnet is uvarovite, which is emerald green with a glassy luster. Garnet is found with either twelve diamond-shaped faces or twenty-four trapezium-shaped faces. It is usually in crystal form and is found in mica, limestone, serpentine, peridotites and granite rocks. Garnet can be located in these rocks, near them on the ground or in streams nearby. They can also sometimes be found near anthills, since ants seem to dislike this mineral and carry it to the surface of the earth. Different forms of garnet can be found in most areas of the United States and other nations of the world.

Since red is the color of Sturgeon people, it is this color of garnet that is most often associated with this moon. Because of its color, the red garnet, like the carnelian, is associated with the heart and the blood. In older times people felt that powdered garnet used as a poultice would act as a stimulant to the heart. Garnet was also believed to warn its owner of danger and ensure a good and honorable life if it was engraved with the figure of a lion. Other peoples believed that a garnet bullet would always penetrate the heart of an enemy. Garnet was also believed to have power to balance sexual energies.

The Romans used to engrave garnets with busts of famous men. Persians considered the garnet regal stones, and so they would engrave the Shah's likeness upon them. Tribes on this continent, too, used the garnet as a ceremonial and jewelry stone.

In contemporary times the garnet, aside from its use in gem jewelry, is also used for a variety of industrial and commercial purposes. Many watches use the garnet as their stones. Pulverized garnets are used as abrasives on paper and are molded into grinding wheels.

The other mineral for Sturgeon people, iron, is one of the hardest of minerals. It is the mineral that brings cultures to the threshold of the technological age and gives them new tools that often destroy their old culture and traditions. Celtic people believe that the Iron Age caused fairies and other magical little folks to turn their backs to humans. Iron does mix well with other minerals and is often responsible for the red color of various gems. Iron is also the central ion in the hemoglobin molecule upon which the human body depends for survival.

Like their minerals, Sturgeon people can be found in a wide variety of forms and settings, yet they have some common characteristics that make them easy to identify. Like the garnet, Sturgeon people are often identified with their hearts, which tend to be large, affectionate and magnanimous. Sturgeon people function best from the feelings that they have in their hearts, and these are usually ones of friendliness and benevolence toward their fellow humans. Because they work from their heart center, they tend to be intuitive and perceptive people who usually have clairvoyant talents, either actively or latently. These talents often make the Sturgeon person aware of danger that might come to him or those close to him, just as the garnet was purported to do.

Because of their perception and sensitivity, these folks have the ability to do and say things that can penetrate straight to the heart of their friends and enemies. Sturgeon people make both powerful friends and powerful enemies. If they feel that you have betrayed them, or those they love, they can turn the full force of their heart energy toward you, in a negative way, and be truly devastating. If they are out of balance, they must guard against their own power, as it can become very impulsive and erratic, causing them to go into true furies that have a very negative effect on their own hearts and circulation. When this happens, they can fall prey to a variety of diseases that further foster their erratic actions.

Like the garnet, Sturgeon people are usually regal in their bearing and attitudes. They stand out in a room full of people because of this trait. Sturgeon folks are usually associated with sexual energies because of their charm and affection, which often arouse sexual feelings in themselves and those around them. From the garnet they need to learn to balance and control these energies so they will not be consumed by them.

People of this moon, like their mineral totems, are useful people in a variety of ways. They are doers who literally will go where angels fear to tread. If you have a difficult task, an impossible job, a truly fearsome responsibility that no one wants to accept, find yourself a Sturgeon person. They are courageous and quite willing to prove that they have this trait. They are versatile and can fit into many fields of employment, culture or philosophy. Just make sure that they believe in whatever they are doing, and you can be assured that they will do it well.

From iron these folks get a certain hardness and an ability to be tempered by their experiences in life. Their association with this mineral further accentuates their connection with the blood and heart. It also accounts for the sometimes sweeping changes these folks can bring to people and projects with which they are associated.

The plant for those born during the Ripe Berries Moon is the red raspberry, that elite and popular member of the berry family. Actually, the raspberry is not a berry but an aggregate of about twenty juicy drupelets. The canes on which they grow are usually erect, freely branched and covered with slender prickles. They grow to three or four feet or more in height, and they are perennial. The leaves are a pale green on top, with a grayish-white color beneath. They have a double serration off a rounded base, and they are usually three inches long and two inches in width. The plants have a white flower that blooms in May, and the berries ripen in June or July for most varieties.

The leaves, roots and berries are considered to be medicinal. The berries are cleansing to the system and, in older times, were considered to be effective for breaking up and expelling gallstones and kidney stones. They were also reputed to stimulate the action of urinary organs.

The root is astringent and has some antibiotic and healing properties because it contains a concentrate of tannic and gallic acid. It has been used as a gargle for sore throats, and the tea, as a compress, has been applied to bleeding wounds and cuts.

A tea made from the leaves has many purposes. It is supposed to help cure diarrhea, especially in infants, and it is an easy tea to give to babies because it has a mild and pleasant taste. It is said to remove cankers from mucous membranes and to tone the tissues involved at the same time. It has many beneficial effects upon the uterus and is frequently drunk by pregnant women to strengthen their uterus, prevent miscarriage and make the birth easier. It is also helpful for female problems during a woman's menstrual cycle. A tea made from the twigs has been used to relieve colds, flu and difficulty in breathing. It can aid in balancing a person's blood sugar level.

From their plant, Sturgeon people can find validation of their status as both elite and popular members of the human family. Like the raspberry, others will often seek them out for the enjoyment that they can provide, even if they are not what they appear to be at first. Sturgeon people, like their berry, often appear to be one way, when, under the surface, they are actually something quite different. This usually works in one of two ways. Some Sturgeon people appear to be all bombastic aggression, rather thorny, when you first encounter them. This prickly outer coating is their way of protecting the soft heart that lurks within. Others appear to be all warmth and affection, but, underneath, you will find a few thorns. This paradox points to another characteristic of the people of this totem. While they are usually friendly and outgoing on the surface, they have a marked tendency to avoid showing their feelings to others. That is the reason they have thorns at one level or another. These help to shield them from any people who want to get beneath their surface and find out what they are truly like.

Beneath the surface, Sturgeon people are very sensitive. Because of their perception, they can easily feel what others are feeling, and this does affect them. They are easily hurt, but they don't like to show this, since it would interfere with the regal, independent, powerful image that they like to project. They will hide their pain or worry behind their friendly, warmhearted show, but they will not readily forget any pain that someone else has caused them, and, in periods when they are out of balance, they will sometimes plot elaborate revenges.

Like the raspberry, Sturgeon people have a cleansing and astringent effect on those around them. In their friendly way they will often kid others out of any fabricated notions that they hold about themselves and the world, thus providing an emotional cleansing of a gentle, yet astringent type. By helping people to cleanse out their false notions, they help to engineer a healing of emotional problems.

Sturgeon people are excellent ones to have around during times of emergency, whether physical or emotional, as their courage is contagious and has helped many to get through serious problems that might have otherwise undone them. In this they are like their plant, which can help to stop bleeding wounds.

Raspberry tea would be beneficial for Sturgeon people to drink at any times when they have colds, sore throats or digestive problems because of their predisposition to heart and circulatory problems. With this predisposition they will stay in better health if they heal themselves of any minor problems before they have the opportunity to turn into something major. And, with Sturgeon people, a small physical upset is often a warning to them that they are getting emotionally out of balance and had better correct the situation before a stronger warning is necessary.

Being born under the Ripe Berries Moon, the second moon of Shawnodese, adds to the warmth of the Sturgeon's external nature. Shawnodese's gift of trust helps them to feel more of this quality within themselves. They need to learn to trust more, on a deeper level, before they can accept his other gift, that of growth. The Ripe Berries Moon is one of openness when all of earth's children are fully opening themselves to the Father Sun and bringing forth the fruit that they are supposed to bear. It is also the month when the warmth of the sun tends always to be evident.

Being of the Thunderbird clan adds to the warmth of Sturgeon folks and to the stability of nature that they most often display to the world. Their clan membership increases their energy and their ability to successfully do a number of things at one time. It increases, too, the necessity for these folks to be careful that they don't overextend themselves and allow their health and energies to deteriorate.

The color of Sturgeon folks is the red of the ripe raspberry or of the prized garnet. This color red signifies the high physical energy, the natural power, the abundance of vital life force and the strong will that Sturgeon people usually have. It is also the color of the heart and the blood, again emphasizing the connection of Sturgeon people with both. This red can also mean erratic action, sensuality, pride, greed and selfishness if the people manifesting it allow the color to be flowing from the less evolved parts of their beings. This red is both a validation and a warning to the people of the Sturgeon. People who have this color have a tendency toward nervous problems, which can lead to deeper problems of the body if they don't take the time to have some periods of quiet when they are involved with things outside of their normal sphere of activities. Some Sturgeon people find it beneficial to sit quietly, reading or meditating, every day, in order to keep their bodies in a good and healthy state. However, being quiet does not come naturally to them and is often a trait that they have to cultivate.

The animal of those born during the Ripe Berries Moon is the sturgeon, the king of fishes. The sturgeon is an old and primitive fish that has probably existed on the earth since about the time that the dinosaur disappeared. The sturgeon, depending on its location and species, comes in a variety of sizes, but can reach twelve-foot lengths and three-hundred-pound weights. The sturgeon has rows of bony plates on his body, making him look like a knight who did not have quite enough time to finish putting on his armor. Fishermen are reported to have said that if sturgeons were completely covered with their plates, it would be necessary to skin them with an ax, which gives you an idea of the toughness of their skin. Sturgeons have a long snout with the mouth on the underside, and four barbels, or sense organs, on the underside of the snout. Their tail lobes are unequal in size, with the upper being the larger. Their skeletons are usually mainly cartilage. They live in the mud bottoms off coasts. Sturgeons usually reach sexual maturity at about twenty years of age, and the females then spawn in spring or early summer, going up streams or moving to shallow water. The female lays two million or more eggs, but probably does not spawn every year.

The most common varieties of sturgeon in this country are the Atlantic sturgeon, the largest species; the shortnose sturgeon; the lake sturgeon, which inhabits the Great Lakes, the upper Mississippi and bays in that area; and the shovelnose sturgeon, the smallest species. Sturgeon species exist across all continents of the northern Temperate Zone.

Sturgeons used to be considered the royalty of fishes among the Native people who inhabited the Great Lakes area. It was the sturgeon who gave Hiawatha a fight for his life and was immortalized in verse for his efforts, bravery and strong heart by Longfellow in his "Song of Hiawatha." All Native people paid respect to this fish. In the Ojibwa nation there is a Sturgeon clan, and it is one of the teaching clans of the nation. To the Ojibwa people the sturgeon represented depth and strength.

Unfortunately, European people did not have the same respect for this fish, first considering it a nuisance when it got in their nets, and later almost fishing it to extinction when they discovered the value of its flesh and its roe, which are better known as caviar. The sturgeon is rare now.

Like their animal totem, people of the Ripe Berries Moon tend to be the ruler of whatever waters they inhabit. They come to this position naturally because of the large amounts of primal energy that run through their beings. They seem to be born to lead, and they are usually fair and benevolent leaders, as long as their energies are flowing smoothly. Their inner strength and clairvoyant abilities help them in knowing what others need and how best to give these things to them. The power that runs through them gives them the energies needed to keep them active and, when necessary, dominant. They have an unending source of inner strength and depth of feelings, as long as they remain harmonious with life. They need always to guard against a tendency to seem arrogant and to be too dominant, as there is a part of them that can enjoy having power over others just for the sake of power. Usually they can protect themselves from power manipulations by being sure to develop their psychic side.

Like the sturgeon, these folks have a tough armor that is very difficult to cut through. They need this when they are in positions of leadership, but they also need to learn to lay their armor aside when they are in relationships that don't require it. If they never let their armor down, they will become too arrogant, and they will not be able to experience the softness and real relating that the sensitive parts of their natures need in order to allow them to grow. They must teach themselves to take off their armor, as it is usually so thick that other people just cannot get through it, even wielding an emotional ax.

It takes years of living before these folks, like the sturgeon, come to the point of maturity where they are able to deal with their own sexual energies. Before this point they can dissipate their vital energies by incorrectly using their sexuality. This is a crucial lesson for Sturgeon people, since they frequently tend to confuse their vital energy with their sexual energy, leading to a misuse of both of them that will often culminate in periods of erratic and destructive behavior.

Sturgeon children have to have limits put upon them when they are young so that they won't wear themselves out before they learn the correct handling of the vital energies flowing through them. But these limits need to be withdrawn as soon as they show the ability to handle their own energies, or they will rebel, usually in very flamboyant and painful ways for themselves and their parents. They are intelligent and active children, but, like those of the Red Hawk, they will usually try to dominate their homes even when they are quite young. They must learn as early as possible that domination is a form of greed that will only cause them pain and confusion.

Sturgeon people make warm and loving parents, but they will often try to dominate their children to the point where the children have no space to develop their own natures in the way that they should. In this instance, the parents must be taught the same lesson that children of this sign need to learn. Sturgeon parents sometimes tire rather quickly of the limitations of parenthood, and, in their efforts to reestablish their own lives in other spheres, they will let go of their children enough that they can have the individual growth that all children need. Sturgeon people are real champions of their children's rights, and they will fervently protect their children from any threats that they perceive. This can sometimes keep the children from developing their own courage and self-reliance.

When people who were born under other totems pass through the Ripe Berries Moon, they can learn about the vital powers that flow through them, sometimes unnoticed. They can learn of the depths of their own courage and strength, and they can experience themselves as leaders of whatever things they are involved in at that time. They can also use their time in this position to experience and balance their own sexual natures and the primal energies that can come through them.

Those of the Sturgeon complement Otter people and are most easily compatible with Red Hawk and Elk people, their elemental clan relations, and with those others of the Butterfly clan, the Raven and Deer people.

Harvest Moon (Brown Bear)
August 23–September 22

Those folks who are born during the Harvest Moon, August 23 to September 22, have the amethyst as their mineral totem, the violet as their plant totem and the brown bear as their animal totem. Their color is purple, and they are of the Turtle elemental clan.

Amethyst is a crystalline form of quartz which is lilac, purple or violet in color and is transparent. It is found in areas all across this country, as well as in many other places in the world. The royal purple stones, which are rarely found, are the most valuable form of amethyst. Amethyst has been popular since early days all over the world. Amethyst rings were often found on the Egyptian pharaohs and on the rulers of the ancient Mayan and Aztec empires. Cleopatra wore a signet ring of amethyst with an engraving of Mithras, the ancient Persian deity. There is an amethyst in the Crown of England, set there by Edward the Confessor.

The amethyst is considered to be symbolic of good judgment, justice and courage. The stone was attributed with the power of protecting its wearer from black witchcraft, as well as lightning and hailstorms. Amethyst was said to have the power to protect its wearer from intoxication. In some countries people made their wine cups from amethyst crystals in the belief that this would keep them from ever becoming drunk.

Other peoples have used the amethyst to help them to achieve spiritual attunement, a good balance between the energies of the physical and spiritual levels.

What an appropriate gem for those of the Brown Bear, who, like their stone, usually show good judgment, justice and courage in their dealings with the world! These folks are ones who exhibit a higher degree of discrimination than people born during other moons. They use their discrimination to reason out any decisions that they make, and their decisions are almost always fair and judicious ones.

Because of their abilities to be fair and analytical, these people are valuable friends and co-workers, ones who are usually popular with all who know them. Like the amethyst, these people have the power to protect themselves and their friends from extremes, whether of alcohol or negativity. Their protection comes largely from their own good sense and their knowing that people make their own negativity and can, therefore, control it if they wish to. Like the amethyst, Brown Bear people can protect themselves and others from lightning and hailstorms, simply because they are the sort of folks who know enough to get in out of the rain.

When they are in a good balance within themselves, Brown Bear people, like their stone, have the ability to help others to achieve a spiritual attunement wherein they can balance their own internal and external energies. Brown Bear people usually make powerful speakers who can help large numbers of people to see the need for a harmony in their own lives. They also make good supervisors and teachers of others, since they tend to be coolly rational, precise in thought and presentation, and accurate in statement. When a Brown Bear person says something you can be sure that they know just what they are talking about.

The color for people of this totem is purple, the color of inspiration, of spiritual insight, of suffering that can lead to a full knowing of the vital creative power of the universe. It is the color of idealism, yet of a practical sort, and of spirituality. It can, in its purer shades, also indicate a love of humanity and an understanding of the need for ritual to help people achieve spiritual understanding. Purple can be a tricky color, though, as its negative shades can connote one who is using spiritual power for personal gain. It is a color of wisdom, whether of positive or negative things.

From their color, Brown Bear people can learn of the highest aspirations to which they can reach and of the pitfalls they might encounter in getting to them. While Brown Bear people are very practical and down-to-earth, a trait that is strengthened by their membership in the Turtle clan, they also have the ability to reach for the things of the spirit if they will allow themselves to do so. Sometimes these folks will limit their reach because their realism gives them an air of cynicism about anything that they cannot actually see. Their sense of reality is the thing that can make them look for "practical" uses of any mystical powers that they uncover. Often "practical" will mean uses that give them personal gain, and, in searching for these, they can misuse the powers they have been given, with bad results for themselves and those around them.

Brown Bear people are born under the last moon of Shawnodese, the Spirit Keeper who represents the qualities of growth and trust. This is an auspicious position for them, since Shawn-odese's gift of growth keeps them from becoming too set in their practical side, while his gift of trust keeps them from becoming too cynical about the world around them and those people who inhabit it with them. Brown Bear people must guard against such cynicism or it will make them become overly critical of everything and everybody. When they swing into such stages, it is difficult to be around them, as there is literally nothing that will help to please or soften them. During such times they can show a marked bitterness totally out of proportion to anything that has happened to them, or they can dredge up every unhappy fact of their lives to justify their feelings.

When Brown Bear people allow themselves to get this far out of balance, they are likely to get diseases that affect their stomach, bowels or heart, and these will often be diseases of blockage, since that is what the unbalanced Brown Bear person is doing to the energy that runs through him or her. If a Brown Bear person in such a state can find a way to release the energy blocks within himself, he will find that it is relatively easy to swing back to a state of good health.

Being born under the Harvest Moon, the moon of the autumn equinox, is helpful to Brown Bear people, as this is the moon when all of earth's children get to reap what they have sown. Knowing that they have a particular affinity for getting back exactly what they put out keeps Brown Bear people from being out of balance too often.

Their Turtle clan membership increases Brown Bear people's ability to remain grounded in the earth while they work on the variety of projects with which they are usually associated. Because they like to be involved with a number of ideas at any time, they don't tend to become so stable that they crystallize in one thing and keep life's energy from flowing through them, a tendency that is more pronounced in people of the other two totems of this clan. Being of the Turtle clan increases Brown Bear people's power and talents.

The plant totem for those born during the Harvest Moon is the violet, that cool forest flower that is often associated with very warm sentiments from the heart. There are four hundred species of violet, most of them perennial, but a few, annual. They are found in damp woods and other shady places. Most grow close to the ground and have dark green rounded leaves, with their well-known delicate violet flowers containing several petals attractively draped over the center septum.

Both the leaves and flowers of violets have been used medicinally, as an antiseptic and expectorant. Because of their mucilaginous properties, they have often been used as a thickener in soups and stews. This is especially true of the variety known as wild okra. People use them to flavor these hot dishes, as well as salads, and they have been made into jams and syrups.

Medicinally, the violet seems to have a property that allows it to reach places normally only penetrated by the blood and lymphatic fluids, and then to dissolve any materials that are toxic. It is a major herb used by Native healers in curing cancer. The tea has been used for difficulty in breathing, especially if caused by toxicity in the stomach or bowels, and for sore throats and tumors of the throat. It will help to cool any high temperature of the body, whether internal or external. It is also useful for ear problems and headaches. It has a general tonic effect on the mucous membranes, much as yarrow does. Used as a compress, it is good for headaches, sore throats, skin problems and toothaches. In some countries the blossoms are burned under abscesses in the belief that the smoke will help to cure any such problems of the skin.

Like the violet, Brown Bear people have a cool quality about them, but this often hides depths of sentiment as tender as those the violet is often used to express. Folks of this totem can feel things strongly, but they often prefer to show their feelings through working to improve the lives of those they love, rather than just talking about their emotions. They are capable of quiet sentimental displays, made more meaningful because of their rarity.

Brown Bear people, like their plant, have both an antiseptic and expectorant quality that they can use. They love the ideas of work and duty and are quick to clean out of their respective organizations any who are not capable of at least paying good lip service to these concepts. If they find that the lip service is only that, they will be equally quick to expel those they see as stopping the progress of whatever it is they are involved with. Brown Bear people like to see concepts and ideas go forward in a strong and steady way, and they will not long abide any who are impeding or undermining their progress. They like to run a clean and tight ship, with everyone's hands honestly on deck.

Like their plant, they also have the capability of penetrating into the secret reaches of the minds and bodies of those around them. If something is wrong with you, don't deny it to your Brown Bear friends. They can see right through your lies, and they won't respect you if they feel that you lie to them often. In fact, if you lie too often, you are liable to feel the full force of their anger, which can be quite strong, though usually expressed in a way that seems cool, perhaps even calculating.

Violet tea could be of use to Brown Bear people when they are experiencing problems of the stomach or bowels. It would also be useful as a compress for the skin problems that sometimes accompany nervous conditions of the stomach and bowels. These folks could use the tea to soothe their throats after they finish the talking at which they are so good.

The animal totem for those born during the Harvest Moon is the brown bear, which is identical to the black bear. In fact, some females will have one brown and one black cub in the same litter. The black bear is more common in the East, while the brown bear is more common in the West. The brown bear, also called the cinnamon bear, is usually four to five feet long, two to three feet at the shoulder, and weighs two to four hundred pounds. They vary in color from blond to all varieties of brown and black, with black ones often having a white or light brown muzzle. They are usually found largely in the West, Alaska and Canada.

They make their dens in holes, caves, beneath fallen trees, deserted buildings or waterfalls. Females tend to line their dens with leaves or grass, while the males do not. They are generally careful and quiet creatures. When excited they will take in a breath while they are giving a bark, and they will also growl, whine and woof. Brown bears are omnivorous, eating anything that they can get their paws on: grass, seeds, plants, vegetables, nuts, fish, ground squirrels, chipmunks, gophers, carrion, garbage.

Their favorite foods are honey and berries. Their only enemies are humans and forest fires.

Bears are curious animals, perhaps more so than any other animal except the raccoon. They lead a slow, deliberate and enjoyable life, taking time to watch and learn from the things that are around them. They only get busy in the fall when they have to eat enough to sustain them through their long winter sleep. The bear's hibernation is not complete. They will sometimes even wake up and go outside on a warm day in the middle of winter, and they are frequently in a half sleep. It is during the latter time of hibernation, which lasts from November until March, that females have their cubs, and so, during the last part of their sleep, they have to be awake enough to nurse them. Bears usually have two cubs, and they weigh about eight ounces, are hairless, and as helpless as baby mice. It takes seven years for a bear to mature. Mother bears are affectionate with their cubs, but they will literally spank them if they do not obey. Male bears do not take part in raising the young.

Bears have a cheerful and good nature, and they will rarely bother humans. They will most frequently flee when they see them, unless it is a mother with cubs, and even then she will make the cubs flee and then dart out herself. The only problem with bears is when they are cornered or are in areas where people have tried to feed and make pets out of them, usually ending up with pests instead. Bears like to eat from human kitchens as the food is easier to get to, and, once they get that habit, it is difficult to break.

Bears can do many of the things that humans do. They can stand on two legs and walk for a short distance, they can climb a tree, usually better than a human can. They can remove honey from a bee tree in an expert way, and they can spear fish, using their claws as spears. To the Native people, the bear was a very special animal. In most legends of the animal world, it is acknowledged that the bear is the head of the council of the animals, because of his fairness, his strength, and his courage. In most tribes the Bear clan was either the medicine, leadership or defense clan.

Like their totem, people of this moon are not terribly home-oriented. They can be comfortable in whatever den they can locate. They do require, however, that, whatever their home, it is reasonably neat and well organized. Brown Bear people can be quiet for long periods of time, and not mind that situation. But when they have something that they feel is important or exciting, they will tell you about it in a very eloquent way. Brown Bear people are usually enthusiastic eaters, like their animal, and they are capable of enjoying a wide variety of foods if they have not committed themselves to a special diet. If they have, they will ardently support whatever this diet is, as perseverance is one of the qualities they cultivate.

Brown Bear people are curious about the world. They like to know what makes everything run, both human and otherwise, especially since this can help them to fix things when they go wrong. They do like to fix up mistakes they see, helping to bring anything into a better balance. These folks are slow and deliberate, taking quite some time before becoming involved with anything new. They also really like to enjoy life and will do everything they can to make their lives comfortable. They also give this consideration to those who are close to them.

Brown Bear people, like their totem, usually slow down in the winter. They like to keep this season slow so that they can contemplate the past year and the one to come. Throughout the year these people tend to be good-natured and cheerful, gentle and confident, as long as they are in a state of balance. If they feel cornered, however, by the circumstances of their lives, by a person or even an idea, they make formidable enemies. They will then come at you and accurately rake any weak spots with their very sharp claws. Because Brown Bear people seem so much a part of this physical reality, people sometimes forget that they are just as comfortable in the spiritual realms and that they have the wisdom from these, as well as the earth. This wisdom allows them to know just where the strengths and weaknesses of other people lie.

Like the Bear, these folks are clever and can do anything they set their minds to, whether or not it is something that usually comes easily to a human. Brown Bear people often become leaders in whatever field they pursue because of their fairness, strength, courage and tenacity. Brown Bear people will hang in there until things become the way they feel that they should be. They also, like the bear, will stringently defend those that they care for, unless they feel that these others need the lesson that meeting the attack will give them.

As parents, Brown Bear women are affectionate, yet strict. They will set their limits on their offspring and expect them to obey. Like the bear, they will leave their young if it is time for their children to be on their own. Brown Bear men, like their totem, are slow to get into parenthood, but usually, they are affectionate parents once they get used to the idea. They tend to swing between strictness and overindulgence. Both demand neatness, order and precision from their offspring, as they don't want children disturbing their tight ship too much.

Brown Bear children are usually gentle and curious, but if they feel that they have been crossed, they will persevere in their show of outrage. They are intelligent children; they often will prefer to be alone for periods of time, as they can easily amuse themselves and as they do have a shy aspect to their nature. It is good for them to learn to have sympathy and compassion for others at as young an age as possible.

When people traveling around the wheel find themselves in this position, they will learn about their own judiciousness, discrimination, analytical and reasoning abilities. They will learn how to balance their own physical and spiritual energies while keeping themselves well grounded on the earth.

Brown Bear people are compatible with their fellow Turtle clan members, those of the Snow Goose and Beaver, and with those of the Frog clan, Flicker, Snake and Cougar people. They complement those of the Cougar.

Ducks Fly Moon (Raven)
September 23 – October 23

Those people born between September 23 and October 23 are born under the Ducks Fly Moon. Their mineral totem is the jasper, their plant totem is the mullein and their animal totem is the raven. Their color is the brown of the autumn earth, and they belong to the Butterfly elemental clan.

Their mineral totem, jasper, is a cryptocrystalline quartz, but not a chalcedony, since it shows a granular rather than a fibrous pattern under an electron microscope. Jasper can come in many colors—brown, reddish brown, black, blue, yellow, green and combinations known as picture jasper. However, the form most directly connected with the people of this moon is the bloodstone, which is green with red spots. Bloodstone is also known as heliotrope.

Bloodstone jasper was known to the ancients of this country, Egypt, Babylon, China and elsewhere. All of these peoples treasured the stone as an amulet, particularly if they found stones that had the shape of a heart. People of older times believed that this form of jasper had the power to give forth the heat of the sun, which accounts for the name "heliotrope," which means "sun-reflecting." People in those days felt that bloodstone jasper placed in water would cause the water to boil.

This stone has many magical powers attributed to it. It is purported to have the power to stop bleeding, to make its owner invisible, to ensure a safe and long life, to draw the poison from snakebite, to restore lost eyesight, to bring rain if placed in water. Until quite modern times physicians used bloodstone to stop bleeding. They would also give it in pulverized form, mixed with egg white and honey, to stop hemorrhage.

This form of jasper, as well as some other forms of the rock, is also believed to give its wearer power over bad spirits and to allow him to cast spells upon others.

All forms of jasper are considered to be stones that give a blessing to their owner, and all forms are said to both possess and attract earth energy. Jasper placed in water and left in the morning sun is thought to have particularly beneficial effects.

Like their stone, Raven people can come in a wide variety of forms, depending upon their mood or balance at any given time. When they are in their proper balance, they are most like the bloodstone, with its wide range of mystical attributes.

Raven people, when they have attained their balance, can be like the most treasured amulet of their stone—all heart. They are kind, loving, considerate and truly concerned with the welfare of others. When they have reached this state, they have the power to absorb the warmth of the sun and to reflect it to all those whom they meet. When they have not found their balance, they, like the bloodstone, have the power to generate depths of depression or confusion that could cause water to boil by their very intensity. Raven people have the tendency to fly from one mood or state to another in an instant, and whichever state they are in seems the best one to them at that particular time. When they find themselves at the opposite pole the next instant, they feel quite comfortable and cannot understand why other people seem confused by their maneuvering.

Like the bloodstone, Raven people have psychic powers, whether or not they have come to the point where they can use them. Sometimes Raven people gain use of these powers before they come to the place of harmony where they will use them wisely. When this happens, Raven people, like their stone, often find that they have the power to influence the lives of others greatly, and they can be tempted to use this power for personal gain. Since Raven people tend to be physically attractive, like the jasper, they can also use this attractiveness to help them when they wish to influence or manipulate those around them. When Raven people are involved in this kind of maneuver, they most often bring pain, confusion and suffering to themselves and those around them.

However, Raven people who have found the point of balance that is within each of them use their special powers for the good of those around them and are often talented healers or mediums for the good forces of the universe.

The jasper is a valuable stone for people of this totem to have around them, because of its ability to attract blessings and the energy of the earth to those who have it. Being of their own nature and of the Butterfly clan, Raven people need to take steps to attract earth energy to them so that they can become better grounded and get on with the proper work of their lives. If they don't do this, they tend, even more than others of this clan, to go from one project to another, never quite accomplishing what they intend to.

The color of Raven people is the brown of the autumn earth, the Earth Mother that has given so much to everything during the summer season of growth, and is readying herself to slow down for a season in preparation for the time of rest and renewal. Brown has the ability to help people unite the power of the earth and the power of the spirit through their own beings. It is the color of being grounded and stable on this plane, while prepared to reach to the realms above. Raven people seek to be in this state and are of great service when they achieve it.

Being born under the first moon of Mudjekeewis, Spirit Keeper of the West, helps Raven people to find their balance, since the gifts of Mudjekeewis are strength and introspection. If Raven people use these gifts to look within themselves, they will come to a point of balance much faster and will then be able to reach out and help others, a goal that they always carry in their hearts. Their moon, the Ducks Fly Moon, is the moon that follows the autumn equinox and brings the season of slowing down from the rapid growth of the season that has passed. If Raven people learn from it to slow themselves down, this, too, will help them to reach their point of balance.

Mullein, the plant totem for those born under the Ducks Fly Moon, is an exceptionally helpful and versatile herb. Mullein is also called velvet leaf, flannel leaf, woolen blanket herb, candlewick plant and velvet dock. These other names help to give a good description of the plant, which has large, light green velvety leaves which grow in a column from a stout, erect, woolly stem. The leaves are basal, narrowing at the base into wings. The plant can grow five or six feet in height and is topped with a spikelike central column, from which its small flowers, usually yellow, red, purple or brownish red, grow. The fruit is a capsule or pod, which also grows from this central spike. Mullein is widely distributed throughout all areas of the United States—both rural and urban—and in many other countries of the world.

Mullein has been widely used for many years in all of the places where it occurs. The leaves can be made into a tea which soothes the mucous membranes, helps relieve bladder, kidney and liver problems, helps in nervous conditions and is a general astringent. Mullein is first thought of as a remedy for problems of the lungs and heart, but, through its soothing action on these organs, it also relieves problems of the kidney and bladder and tones the nervous system. Natives here smoked the leaves of the mullein, rather than tobacco, in many areas. When smoked, this herb helps to relieve lung congestion and its resultant maladies, such as asthma and bronchitis. The leaves were also burned as an incense to relieve these conditions.

Oil made from the mullein flowers has long been used as eardrops, as a wart remover and to relieve bruises, sprains and chapped skin. Externally the tea is used to treat hemorrhoids, ulcers, tumors, swelling of the throat and muscle tenderness. In older days mullein was also credited with having antibiotic qualities.

From the mullein plant, Raven people are again reminded of their many versatile and helpful talents, as well as their ability to shift and change. Some of the names of the mullein plant are good descriptions of these folks in their various stages of being, for they can be as scratchy as wool one day and as soft as velvet the next. When they are in their woolen stage, they are sometimes difficult to be around, as they are scratching themselves as well as others, and require large amounts of attention to help them get over the soreness that they feel. When they are like velvet, they are soothing and gentle and a pleasure to be near. When Raven people like themselves, they are capable of making other people feel simply wonderful. They will go far out of their way to show those around them how very special they are and how lovable. In contact with such a Raven person you will feel like you are the nicest, most important person in the world. And you will love them for making you feel so good.

Raven people, like the mullein, can be very soothing to any ills that you have, no matter what the cause. Their true concern will often give you the push that you need to get on the road to recovery. When they are in a good frame of being, they will generously listen to all of your problems and really try to help you to solve them, or at least feel better about them. Their openheart-edness will sometimes make you feel as though you really don't have any problems at all. Like their plant, they can soothe you, often in a very physical way by hugging or caressing, for Raven people do like to give and receive physical affection.

People of this totem would do well to keep some mullein around for their own use, as they are prone to problems with their bladder and kidneys, as well as nervous conditions. Mullein can help to relieve all of these. Raven people seem to get these problems only when they are in states where they have lost touch with their central balance. At such times they get high-strung, irritable and given to paranoid thoughts, and, if they are not able to bring themselves back into balance, physical problems such as those described above are likely to ensue.

The animal totem for those born during the Ducks Fly Moon is the raven. The raven is usually an all-black bird with a wedge-shaped tail. The raven is as large as a red hawk, about twenty-five inches in length, with a wingspread of up to fifty-four inches. The wings are long and pointed, the bill is large and heavy and the nostrils are covered by bristly feathers that are called filoplumes. Ravens usually have a tuft of feathers at their throat, and, in the species known as the white-necked raven, this tuft is white, although the white can only be seen when the feathers are blown by the wind or when the ravens are courting. Ravens are found all over the world but are most often found in this country in the western states. Their song is a loud croak. They are omnivorous, eating vegetables, small mammals, young birds, garbage and carrion. Their flight pattern is a "flap, soar, flap" one, and they are capable of riding the winds with as much enjoyment as their hawk brothers. Their aerial displays are particularly dramatic during their mating season.

Ravens are sometimes aggressive, but most often wary. They are intelligent birds who know enough to drop shellfish from the air in order to break the shells and get the flesh that is inside. Ravens are group-oriented and very defensive of their territory. They will attack hawks, owls and even eagles who intrude upon their space. The gypsy people particularly admire crows and ravens for their loyalty to their tribe. It is said that these birds have tribal councils, and, if you have ever seen a flock of them sitting on a fence or pole talking with each other, you might suspect that this is the truth. It is even said that if these birds go against the laws of the tribe, they will commit suicide by dropping from a high place.

Some ravens pair for life; others don't. They build large nests of sticks on ledges or near the tops of trees. They lay five to seven eggs, which are greenish, spotted with brown. Ravens fly with their mouths open during hot weather.

To the Native people, ravens are thought of as birds of balance between man and nature. Almost all tribes have a legend about the raven, explaining why he is black. In all of these legends the raven begins as a white bird whose color was changed either as a punishment for wrongdoing or in an effort to help man, usually by trying to put out a fire that threatened the people. This duality in the legends illustrates the duality that Native people feel about the raven. To some, the raven is a bad omen; to others, a good one. To the Pueblo peoples the raven is connected with the kachina spirits, the spirits that protect the villages and bring the rain. Ravens have been attributed both with bringing the dark clouds that yield the rain and with holding them away. They also have been credited with bringing the game and with holding that away. Whatever the tribal position, the raven was seen as a bird that was intimately linked with the world of humans and nature.

Like the raven, people of this totem are capable of soaring to and fro and of winging down to a place where they can absorb the good energy of the earth. They are people who are comfortable in both the realms of the earth and the realms of the sky. How far they can fly and how gracefully they can soar depend on the state of balance that they have achieved within themselves. More than with the other totems of the Medicine Wheel, a state of balance is crucial for those of the Raven, because, like their bird, they are capable of quickly soaring from one position to another. If they have not come to the point of knowing themselves enough to know where their center point really is, this soaring can be exceptionally confusing to them and the people around them. When they have achieved this balance, they are capable of soaring from one realm to another, without ever losing sight of their own center. Raven people in this condition are some of the most helpful people that you can know. Since they have suffered to get to this point of harmony, they are capable, and willing, to help others achieve it.

The Raven totem is a paradoxical one, because Raven people exemplify the paradoxes of life in their own emotions. Because they are capable of soaring high, they can see both the good and the bad in any viewpoint, and it is sometimes very difficult for them to see that one is really preferable to another. They are not quick to make decisions, until they have come to harmony. Before this, the decision of one day will often change by the next. Because of this, they frequently appear indecisive and, sometimes, irresponsible.

Like their bird, Raven people are wary, and with good reason, as they have probably been hurt by being gullible in the past. They will tend to withdraw from a situation at any sign of danger. They are intelligent people, able to learn from all of the views and ideas that they are capable of seeing. They are, because of their natures, quite adaptable. Since they are so used to living in an emotional world of change, changes in the physical world don't bother them greatly.

Raven people tend to be group-oriented. They are happiest when they are with a group of people who share enough of their ideas that they can feel secure. When they have found such a group, they will be very cooperative with it and loyal to it. They will also, like their bird, exhibit a spirit of defensiveness about this group and its territory, whether it is philosophical or literal. If they feel that those they love are threatened, they will defend them against anything else, whatever its size or strength. Because of their group loyalty, they feel very bad if anything happens that makes them go against a group that they have joined. Such a situation will knock them temporarily off balance, no matter how centered they are.

Like their totem, some Raven people pair for life, while others don't. If they have chosen a mate before they have come to know the harmony within themselves, they sometimes find it difficult to keep up the relationship, as they frequently change their mind about whether or not they have chosen the right partner. Their constant ambivalence is enough to drive off any but the most determined mate.

The home is important to these folks. They have an eye for

attractive settings, and they like to be sure to place themselves in one. Having the proper home is often an important factor in determining when Raven people will come into a state of harmony. It is also important for Raven people to have animals in their household, as this is one concrete way in which they can experience the link they have with nature.

As parents, people of this totem are very warm, loving and soothing. However, they find it difficult to be consistent with their children, as their feelings about discipline can change as quickly as their feelings on anything else. Of course, the balanced Raven person is an exception to this, and usually is a model parent, giving their children the correct balance of love, discipline and independence.

Raven children, unless they are truly exceptional souls, usually have some difficulty, as they must test all possible ways of being in order to determine how they want to be. They should be given some leeway to do this, as it will help them to find their balance later in life, but they need consistency from those around them in order to experience the peace that this can bring to others. They are always very loving children, often very physically beautiful and always ready for a hug and kiss.

When Raven people have reached their personal balance, they have the ability to seek out all kinds of hidden things, both on this plane and others. At this point, Raven people are able to personify the paradoxes of living, without being thrown by them. They are capable of teaching others how to combine the energy of the earth and the sky within themselves, and, by so doing, they help to bring about a balance between man and nature, just as the Native people credited ravens with doing.

People traveling around the wheel who find themselves in this position will find that they can experience the paradoxes of their own lives in a much more direct and intense way than they have before. By experiencing them, they will often find that they are more capable of resolving them. They may discover how they can help to bring about a balance between themselves and nature. And they can explore their feelings about participating in, and being loyal to, any groups with which they have wanted to become involved.

Raven people are compatible with their relations in the Butterfly clan, the people of the Otter and Deer, and with those of the Thunderbird clan, people of the Red Hawk, Sturgeon and Elk. They find their complement in the Red Hawk people, the winged ones of the Thunderbird clan.

Freeze Up Moon (Snake)
October 24–November 21

Those born during the Freeze Up Moon, October 24 until November 21, have copper and malachite as their mineral totems, the thistle as their plant totem and the snake as their animal totem. Their color is orange, and they are members of the Frog elemental clan.

Their mineral, copper, is found all over the world, and, since the earliest times when people learned how to work it, it has been used for implements of all kinds and for ornamentation. In its earliest periods of use copper is usually pounded into the desired shape. In later time it is smelted and formed. Copper is attributed with a wide variety of special powers. Basically it is thought to help with purification of the spirit and the blood. For untold years people who have had problems with arthritis or rheumatism, or with any diseases that cause stiffening of the joints, have used bracelets or anklets of copper to bring them relief. Artists often wear bracelets of copper to keep their arms from stiffening, and warriors have used bracelets or armbands of this mineral to strengthen their arms.

Copper conducts electricity better than most other minerals, and so it is used almost always in wiring for this energy. It also causes heat to spread evenly over a surface, which is the reason for copper, or copper-bottomed, pans. In older times copper was also considered a conductor for other types of energy. It was frequently the metal used in combination with crystals that had powers to focus energies that our sciences have yet to discover.

Malachite, the gemstone for Snake people, is a copper carbonate, found where copper mining is taking place. It is bright green in color, with a luster that can range from glassy to dull or silky. Clear specimens of malachite have been used as gems and also have been carved into vases, ornaments and statues. Like copper, malachite is found in most areas in this country. This stone is thought to have particular spiritual powers. Most important, it is said to raise a person's sensitivity to the voice of the spirit. It is considered a stone that increases your receptivity to all forms of subtle energy and increases your psychic powers.

From their stones, Snake people can learn of their own abilities to transmute the things with which they come in contact. Like copper, Snake people have the ability to bring change to any of the things with which they are involved. While they are usually not very malleable themselves, they can adapt situations around them into whatever shapes they desire. Snake people have high energy running through them at most times, and they have many new ideas about ways in which any situation can be improved. When they are in good balance, most of their ideas will be sound ones, and ones they are fully capable of implementing.

Because Snake people are generally attuned to the higher energies around them, once they have purified their own spirits they are capable of helping others with this task. Since many of them are natural healers, they can help people to purify their bodies and their blood. Like copper, they help to keep stiffness or weakness away from those with whom they associate by the strength and power of their own energy.

Snake people, like copper, are very capable of conducting the higher energies that surround all of us. They naturally have a grasp of other realms that are spiritual as well as material. Because of their inquisitive, investigative natures, they are able to bring the knowledge of these realms into a form that is easily understood by other people. Like copper, Snake people also have the ability to spread heat evenly, be it the heat of their newest ideas or the heat of their wrath when things are going in a manner that they find displeasing.

Like the malachite, Snake people do have particular spiritual powers. When in balance, they are very sensitive to the voice of spirit, able to receive many kinds of subtle energies. Snake people are gifted in the psychic realms, no matter what their state of general development. This gift can be either a blessing or very detrimental to them if they have not bothered to develop themselves into the type of people who know that such gifts should be used for the good of humankind, not for their own personal gain. Snake people who do use these powers for their own purposes can be very successful at doing so, and they can sway large numbers of people to their way of thinking, but they will ultimately undo themselves when they get a clear look at what they are really doing. And, being as closely related to spirit as they are, such a look will inevitably come to them.

The plant totem for the Snake people is the thistle, that sharp-spined plant that grows in most places in both the city and the country. The thistle can grow from three to ten feet high. It has a thick taproot, which resembles a carrot. During its first year the leaves grow in a rosette, and the flowering stem grows during the second year. The stem is thick and succulent, sometimes with leaves and branches. The flower heads are loose clusters, and the flowers can be red, purple or white. The leaves and flowers are all covered with very sharp, prickly hairs, and a bristly down covers every part of the plant. If you accidentally brush by a thistle, you will know it.

The young stem can be peeled and eaten raw or cooked, and so can the root. The young leaves are harvested for use as a tea, and the fruitlike seeds can be eaten either raw or roasted. All parts of the thistle are rich in minerals. Traditionally, Native healers used the thistle for weakened stomachs and digestive problems, for reducing fevers, for expelling worms and for increasing the milk in nursing mothers. In older times the thistle was considered an all-purpose herb capable of curing most maladies known to man, particularly those of the brain. It was alleged to strengthen all of the internal organs of the body and to help to cure all sorts of aches and pains. Some species of the thistle are called holy thistle or blessed thistle because of the healing qualities attributed to them.

Snake people, like their plant, can mentally and emotionally grow to a great or small height, depending upon their willingness to properly cultivate and use the talents and abilities that lie within them. From the thistle, Snake poeple can learn of the importance of their having a strong and deep root into the earth, for they need the help of the earth in order to learn to properly channel all of the energies that run through them. While all Snake people have the ability to be very helpful to the world around them, some of them lose this opportunity because they, like their plant, cover themselves with such prickly spikes that few people are able to get close enough to see the good things that are beneath this outer coating. Even well-harmonized Snake people usually have a little coating of bristly down that will stick into anyone they feel has injured them or those they love.

If you succeed in getting past the outer coating of a Snake person, you will find that what lies within is as multipurpose and valuable as the thistle is alleged to be. Snake people can help to cleanse and heal their own body or those of others through their powers to discern what the malady really is. Then they can direct their healing abilities, either of a scientific or other nature, toward it.

Snake people can use their plant to help keep all of their internal organs in order, since they are prone to problems with their blood system and all that it touches when they are not in a good balance. During such times they will also be prone to all the varying types of nervous maladies that can affect people, from ulcers to fits of depression. When Snake people are in a weakened and confused condition, they need to first bring their own energies into balance before any other type of treatment can be totally effective. Since they are regenerators, they are quite capable of doing so once they determine that they want to. If they will not make this decision, it is difficult for anyone else to help them.

It is Snake people in a confused condition who are the sharpest and thorniest of this totem. They are quite capable of being stubborn, critical, jealous, deceitful and given to times of furious anger, often cuttingly directed toward those who are closest to them. It is important for Snake people in this condition to remember that they have all the power they need to bring their energies into a more helpful, pleasant, clear and serving place.

The color of the people of the Snake totem is orange, that special clear orange that is occasionally seen in the sunset sky. This is a color that symbolizes one who is vital, intellectual and capable of applying any knowledge that they glean from life or study. It is a color that shows that the person can understand mind, body and spirit, and can use his highest understanding to control his lower ones. It is also a color that signifies an ambitious person and one who takes pride in the work he does. All of these qualities are ones exhibited by those of the Snake totem. These folks are intellectual, or capable of being so. They have the ability to observe life keenly and the lessons it gives them, and to apply these lessons to their own lives and the lives of others. They have intense self-control, if they choose to use it, and they are ambitious and proud of all that they accomplish.

Snake people are born during the Freeze Up Moon, the second moon of Mudjekeewis to the West. Since they are also of the Frog clan, the clan of the water, their moon gives them a warning

---

about what can happen to them if they allow their energies to run undirected. Doing this, literally, will cause them to freeze up, to be unable to allow more energies to come within them. This moon also tells them that sometimes it is necessary for them to freeze up their energy purposely for a time until they feel clear enough to deal with it.

Mudjekeewis, who brings the gifts of introspection and strength, is a very appropriate Spirit Keeper for these folks, as he has the ability to help them expand the strength and self-searching that is already theirs by nature. Being of the Frog clan tends to soften Snake people, to allow them to experience emotions that their intellectuality would otherwise try to deny them. While they are of the water, they are of clear, deep lakes, rather than wildly running streams or rivers. They are not as easily changeable as their other relations in this clan.

The animal totem for people born during the Freeze Up Moon is the snake, that old, mysterious, maligned and misunderstood member of the Vertebrata family. The snake, or serpent, is a limbless reptile with expandable jaws, slender, inwardly-sloping teeth set toward the back of the mouth, no ear openings or movable eyelids. The back of the snake contains many vertebrae, sometimes up to three hundred. The ribs are loosely attached to the vertebrae to allow the snake to loop itself around, which is part of the way in which it moves. It also has a large row of belly scales, called scutes, each overlapping the one behind it, with its free edge pointing backward. By reaching forward with each scute, while pressing backward, the snake is able to glide.

The forked tongue of the snake is a very delicate instrument able to give its owner the senses of both taste and smell. What the tongue picks up is analyzed by a special organ on the roof of the mouth. Snakes have an excellent sense of smell and, generally, of sight. The exception to this is in the period before the snake sheds its skin, when the eyes seem dull and cloudy, since the skin over them is part of what is shed. Snakes shed their skins about three times a year. They fasten onto something at about chin level and glide out of the old skin. It is at the time of shedding that rattlesnakes, the most common of our pit vipers, add a new rattle to their tail.

In the world there are close to 2,500 species of snakes. In the

United States there are 114. That is a pretty good track record for an animal that has been around since the Cretaceous period, when the dinosaurs were ready to leave. During many of these years snakes have been hunted by man out of misunderstanding and unnecessary fear.

Snakes are carnivorous, mainly eating small animals like rats and frogs. They will also eat insects, like flies and mosquitoes. Because of their diet preferences, they are an essential part of the balance of nature, and, where man has wantonly murdered snakes, he is often overrun by rats and mice. In ancient Greece and Rome snakes were used as mousetraps. Snakes digest slowly and may be sluggish for a week after eating. Their meals can exceed 50 percent of their own body weight.

Snakes are very adaptable to their environment. They are exquisitely sensitive to touch and vibrations, partly because they are cold-blooded and are dependent upon their environment for warmth. They change their colorations to blend with the land that surrounds them. Snakes have no voice, but some can hiss, and rattlesnakes can buzz their rattles. Despite their cold-blooded reputation, the courtship of snakes is a very warm affair. Females secrete a particular musky scent to attract a male, who approaches her slowly and rubs his nose all over her body. When the female responds, they throw casual loops over each other and finally mate when they are so entwined they are almost indistinguishable.

Females are both live-bearing and egg-laying, and most young snakes are born during the warm summer months. Many never have any contact with the parents. Snakes do hibernate in the winter. The most feared snakes are the pit vipers, those who have a pit between their nostrils which enables them to pick up the warmth of any animal they are tracking. They also have a special gland attached to their eyeteeth through which they shoot venom, usually into animals intended for a meal. Most snakes, even those of the poisonous varieties, avoid contact with humans and will strike only in self-defense. If you find yourself in a snake's territory, the best thing to do is to calmly and quickly move out of it.

While many European myths put the snake in a rather unpopular position, the snake was respected in most Native cultures.

The feathered serpent was the foremost symbol of the ancient Mayan and Aztec empires, representing the transforming powers that their religions gave them. The Hopi people feel that the snake is a messenger from other realms and has the capacity to bring the life-giving rains. The Ojibway people feel that the snake represents patience, since he is so slow to anger, and the Snake clan was one of their medicine clans. Most other tribes also attribute special powers to the snake, and many have Snake clans that perform special functions.

Like their totem, people of the Freeze Up Moon also tend to be mysterious and secretive. It takes them quite some time to open to other people, and even then, they are frequently reluctant to reveal the secrets of their innermost being. Because of this, and because of their tough, prickly outer covering, these folks are sometimes misunderstood and even maligned. They have so much vital energy flowing through them that other people sometimes can't understand the depths of their being. Like the snake, people of this totem also have delicate instruments for sensing, tasting and smelling out the truth about people and situations. They have keen eyes that enable them to see through to the depths of the soul, whether it is their own or another's. The exception to this, for Snake people, is the time in which they feel confusion and don't allow their force to flow smoothly through them.

Snake people are useful in maintaining the balance of nature, or the balance of any situation, when they themselves feel a good harmony within. They are adaptable people, and, like their animal totem, they have the ability to shed their old skin of ideas, environment or feelings, when it is time for them to transform themselves into a new phase of being. Change doesn't always come easily to these folks, but, when it does, it is permanent until it is time for them to go into something new.

Like the snake, people of this totem are not cold-blooded when it comes to relationships. Because of all the vital force that comes through them, they tend to be highly sexual beings. When they are in balance, they can utilize their sexual energy in good and loving ways, but, when out of balance, this energy sometimes seems to be the controlling force of their lives, and they have great difficulty in rechanneling it. Whatever their inner state, Snake people are reputed to be intense and exciting lovers.

As parents, Snake people are sometimes too cold-blooded toward their children. They will let their children take over the reins of their lives before they have the wisdom and experience to do so. They are so involved in their own lives that they don't want to stop their own transformation to give their children the emotional things they need. At other times Snake people are very warm toward their children, giving them all that they can of their time and energy. This gliding from one position to another is confusing to their offspring, although some Snake people adopt one or the other position and don't vacillate from it.

Snake children are interesting and intelligent, but sometimes difficult to handle, since they seem to have a wisdom beyond their years. They also tend to be secretive and sometimes cold, not showing the affection that people expect from youngsters. If they are not shown how to begin channeling their energy, they will get into phases of furious temper, which is very hard to control.

The Native American view of the snake is much more relevant to people of this totem than the European one that many of us grew up with. Snake people are worthy of respect because of the power to transform that they carry within them. They can be messengers, bringing messages that we all need to hear, if we learn to get close enough that we can hear them. These folks can also demonstrate remarkable patience in their teaching of others if they have learned to keep their own energies in balance.

When people from other totems travel through this position on the wheel, they can learn of their own power to transform their innermost beings, bringing all of the lessons they have learned in other positions into harmony. They can also learn of their own adaptability, patience, tenacity, ambition and power. People from the Snake totem, or passing through it, are often those capable of performing heroic deeds to help their fellow children of our common Earth Mother.

Snake people are compatible with their fellow Frog clan members, those of the Cougar and Flicker, and with those of the Turtle clan, Snow Goose, Beaver and Brown Bear people. They particularly complement those of the Beaver clan.

Long Snows Moon (Elk)
November 22–December 21

People born during the Long Snows Moon, November 22 until December 21, have the obsidian as their totem in the mineral kingdom, the black spruce as their totem in the plant kingdom and the elk as their totem in the animal kingdom. Their color is black, and they are members of the Thunderbird elemental clan.

Obsidian, the mineral for Elk people, is also known as volcanic glass. Chemically, it is identical to granite, containing feldspar, quartz and ferromagnesiums. If granitic magma solidifies beneath the surface, granite is formed. If the same magma pours rapidly out onto the earth and cools quickly, it becomes obsidian. Sometimes you can find mountains of this mineral. If the magma cools rapidly, but not quick enough to become shiny, it results in a mineral called pitchstone, which has a dull luster. Small, rounded pieces of obsidian which weather out of larger masses are called Apache tears. Obsidian is usually black, shiny and translucent, although it is sometimes found in other colors, and one variety shows enough colors that it is referred to as rainbow obsidian. Obsidian is hard and razor-sharp along its edges, so it should always be handled carefully. It is found in most of the western states in the United States.

Obsidian has long been used by the Natives of this continent. The Mayans formed obsidian into mirrors and into extremely intricate jewelry including cylinder earplugs so thin they are transparent as glass. They, along with the ancient Egyptians, also carved obsidian into statues and other decorative pieces. That is quite a feat considering that obsidian is one of the most difficult minerals to work, because of its hardness and extreme tendency to crack. In North America the Native people formed obsidian into arrowheads, spearheads and scrapers, as well as jewelry.

Because of its origin deep within the breast of the Earth Mother, obsidian is thought to have the power to ground people to the earth energy, teaching them how to respect and use this energy within. Obsidian is thought to have the power to reflect the thoughts of another person to the one who is wearing it, bestowing upon the wearer a sort of clairvoyance. Because of this ability, obsidian has often been used as a scrying stone, one that allows people to see into the future. Scrying stones would be formed by breaking obsidian and finding a smooth surface in which to stare. Obsidian is also attributed with the power to protect its wearer or holder against evil spirits.

Like their mineral, Elk people can be both shiny and translucent. When they are well developed in their natures, they have an inner glow that lights their entire beings. They also have the ability to let you see somewhat into their beings, but no more deeply than they wish you to look. Elk people, like their stone, can be hard to shape to a new viewpoint or situation, but, once they are there, they will be there solidly. They walk a razor's edge in their lives, as their nature is one of duality.

Like obsidian, people of this totem make good mirrors for other people, when they are clear themselves. At this point in their development, Elk people can reflect to another what his or her inner state really is. Elk people have the ability to cut through a lot of outer impressions and get to the heart of most matters, much as the arrowheads made from their mineral do. Elk people can benefit from wearing their mineral because they can use the greater knowledge of earth energy that obsidian can give to them.

Well-developed Elk people, like their stone, have the ability to be clairvoyant and to transmit thoughts. They also will protect those to whom they are close from any dangers that they perceive, whether on the material level or on other levels.

The black spruce, the plant totem for the Elk people, is a majestic member of the pine family that grows in many regions throughout the United States. The spruce can grow to more than forty feet in height, tapering upward to a point. Its bark is a combination of dark browns and black, and the needles are dark green, arranged in compact spirals around the twigs. Each needle is four-sided and looks nearly square in cross section. The cones, which hang straight down, mature in one season. The branches are horizontal, often drooping. The wood is soft, strong and free from knots.

The tips of the tree, when young, are aromatic. They can be nibbled or made into tea. Either way they have a high vitamin C content. Evergreens were the oranges of the Natives. The gum of the spruce is the medicinal part that has been used by people here for hundreds of years as an antiseptic and to loosen mucus in the throat and chest. The gum can be applied to cuts and wounds to clean them. It can be made into a plaster for setting bones and used on the face to protect it from sunburn. A tea from the twigs makes a good bath and is also helpful in curing colds. The gum can be used as an inhalant, both in and out of the sweat lodge.

Some tribes would eat the cambrium layer between the bark and the wood in the spring or dry it into cakes for winter. Some used the cambrium only as a laxative agent. Other tribes would harden the spruce pitch in cold water and chew it for pleasure, as we do chewing gum today.

From their plant totem, Elk people can learn about the majestic bearing that is theirs when they learn to come into balance and harmony with all of the possibilities and gifts that have been given to them. Like the wood of their tree, Elk people can be soft and strong at the same time. Theirs is an inner strength that can allow them always to follow the proper direction and to lead others onto the path most suited to them. It is not a strength that requires a hardness of nature, a quality that would not suit the warm, courteous and sometimes conventional character of these folks.

Like the spruce, Elk people can be both antiseptic and loosening. They have an innate sense of justice, and they will try to clean out anything they sense as unjust from any situation. With their intuitiveness they are also able to see into the hearts of others and help them loosen any of the hard knots they have allowed to come into their beings.

The spruce tree might be of use personally to people of this totem during times when they hurt their knees and thighs, areas of particular vulnerability to them. At these times, the plaster property of spruce gum might be a handy thing for them to know. During times when they are not as vulnerable, they might benefit from either chewing or inhaling the spruce gum, to make certain they keep their throats working well. Since Elk people sometimes like to teach and expound to others, they will find this herb useful when their voice is getting weak from overwork.

Elk people are born under the Long Snows Moon, the third moon of Mudjekeewis. They, like the others of this direction, benefit from the gifts of introspection and strength that Mudjekeewis gives. Since, by their nature, they are thoughtful people, the additional introspective powers that Mudjekeewis gives helps them have more ability to look within themselves and within others. Being born under the Long Snows Moon, the beginning of the time when all of earth's children prepare for their season of renewal, gives Elk people ever more ability to seek out and use the thoughts that flow through them. Their connection with this time of year helps them to temper the energy that comes to them as members of the Thunderbird clan. They are the least fiery, or longest burning, members of this clan, because of their time of birth. The time of snow moderates the amount of their flame, without ever putting it out.

The color associated with the people of the Elk is the black of the night falling upon the earth. This dusky black is a time when things are in their formless state, when the activities of the day surrender themselves to the introspection of the evening. It is the formlessness from which all things can come, the void that contains all things, as well as nothing. This black gives Elk people the power of surrender that can allow their intuition, their inner knowing, to come through and guide their lives. It is the black mystery preceding the time when all things can become known. It is the time when you must look within, not without, for answers to the questions that life poses for you. To Native people here, black is one of the sacred colors, signifying the strength and looking within of Mudjekeewis to the West. It is a color of learning, not of negativity.

The animal totem for those born under the Long Snows Moon is the elk, that most regal member of the deer family. The elk, also known as wapiti, is the largest of the deer family and, to many people, the most beautiful. Its antlers, which resemble the branches of a tree, are shed annually. The male elk, known as a bull, can reach a length of nine and a half feet and a height of five feet. He can weigh up to 750 pounds. In the summer elk have a coat of light brown, with darker head and limbs. The rump is buff, the hair is short and the mane seems thin. In the winter the elk becomes a grayish brown, with dark head and limbs. At this time the mane becomes longer, fuller and darker. Calves are brown, with light spots, until early in the fall.

Elk live in the woodlands, going to the high country in the

summer and coming back to lower lands in the fall and winter, when it is more difficult for them to find the food they need. Like the deer, the elk lives on grass, leaves, twigs and bark. In some areas there will be elk lines on trees where the elk have eaten as far up a tree as their head can reach. During the time of heavy snow, when it is difficult for elk to find any food, they will sometimes eat from farm haystacks. It is nearly impossible for a farmer to keep an elk out of his hay unless he puts it up on a platform. Wooden and barbed-wire fences do very little to stop a hungry and determined elk. What farmers object to is the elk's habit of getting on top of a haystack and then pulling it apart, as though they expected to find the really good things at the bottom.

For most of the year, elk, like deer, live in herds composed of members of their own gender. They seem to have a good sense of responsibility for each other. When snows are heavy, they will take turns at breaking the trail, and, if you follow the trail of a herd, it will often resemble the trail of a single elk; they are that careful to step into the tracks of the groundbreaker. Elk sometimes seem to dance together, forming a big circle, in which they prance around and sometimes break into a gallop of joy. Elk are fast animals, able to go at thirty miles an hour for short distances. They are also able to leap fences close to ten feet high.

Elk have few natural enemies. Cougars, bears and wolves will sometimes succeed in bringing down a calf, or a weak or sick animal, but none of them are a match for the bull in his prime. Before 1900, however, most of the elk in this country were slaughtered by hunters, who often only wanted two of their teeth to make into jewelry. Others wanted their heads as parts of their trophy collection. When the population was close to decimated, stronger laws protecting elk were put into effect, and we imported many elk from Canada in order to restock the population in this country.

In October, when the mating season is about to begin, bull elk come into prime. They have full antlers, their shoulders swell, their coats and manes are full and they look like the king of the deer. They come forth trumpeting their challenge to any other bulls in the area. During this time they also bugle and whistle. Following the challenge of the bugle call, two elk emerge from the forest and rush toward each other with all of the anger they can manage. They crash together and fight until one succeeds in knocking the other off its feet and then gores him. These battles are more fierce than those of the male deer, but usually are not fatal. To the winner goes the spoils, in this case, the watching cow. Unlike the deer, elk try to get as many cows as they can into their harem, and they will fervently defend them from the approaches of any other male.

When it is time to calf, in the spring, the cows go to the valleys, while the bulls move to higher country to protect their antlers, which are in the delicate velvet stage. Calves are hidden for the first part of their lives during the times when their mothers go out to browse. Like fawns, they are born without a smell to afford them further protection. They are able to go with her at six weeks, but they aren't weaned until the fall, and they sometimes stay with the mother for half a year after that. Most elk only have one calf at a time.

Like their animal totem, Elk people look like they are members of some royal family. They have a proud and straight bearing and an air of majesty that surrounds them when they are functioning well. Since they are insightful, introspective and capable of absorbing much of what they read, hear, see or experience of life, they are often found in the position of a teacher of some sort, where their regal air attracts students to them. Elk people use this attraction well, in most cases, bringing the students in through it, and then sharing generously of what they have learned. Whether they choose to be teachers or not, Elk people are very watchful for others, truly concerned about the welfare of those around them.

Elk people are very aware of justice, both as a concept and a practice, and they are very impatient with anything that they sense is an injustice. When they come across anything that falls into this latter category, they will trumpet their discovery loudly, so that all those involved will know about it and, hopefully, will try to correct it. If those involved do not take action, the Elk person will trumpet even louder and will continue doing so until something has happened to change the situation. If this trumpeting is coming from a well-balanced Elk person, it is usually beneficial to all of those involved. If it is coming from an Elk who has yet to find his clarity and intuition, it can create havoc, and unnecessarily.

Like their totem, Elk people like to go to the high places, either physically or otherwise. Their insightful minds are able to open doors that allow them to soar into realms that others avoid. Their intuition tells them when they are ready to make such flights and when it is necessary for them to come back to their grounding in the earth plane. Like the elk, it is necessary for folks of this totem to come sometimes into the lowlands and valleys in order for them to remain harmonized with the things that surround them. While Elk people have natural spiritual gifts and the ability to teach these to others, they must have grounding or they will not use these gifts in the best manner that they can. Elk people have a very independent streak, although they are willing to take leadership from others if it is of the proper kind for them at that time.

Sometimes Elk people retreat to the high country of their minds too frequently, using these journeys to avoid having any real contact with others. Elk people try to keep themselves closed about the things that are deeply within their spirits, and they sometimes fear relationships that might cause them to truly open to another. At this point, they will retreat from the relationship in mind if not in body.

While they tend to be closed about their deep feelings, they appear to be very warm and openhearted on the surface. This duality can sometimes cause real pain for Elk people and for those who love them. They will seem warm, loving and totally supportive of everything around them one day, and they will decide to leave the whole situation the next. Elk people are not given to quick changes of heart. They just don't know how to express dissatisfaction until it gets to the point where it cascades out into what seems like a sudden move.

Once an Elk person has made up his mind to do something, it is very difficult to change it. They are determined individuals and fearless when they are convinced that they are right. Like the male of their totem species, they are also able to be flamboyantly argumentative, and, when they are in this state, it is virtually impossible to win an argument with them. If Elk people allow their argumentativeness or the closed part of their natures to become dominant, they will be prone to illnesses that show up as stiffness in some part of the body. To cure themselves, they must stop blocking the giving, understanding and loving energy that can flow through them. Like the elk, these folks do have a playful side of their nature that enjoys dancing, singing and just having fun. If they develop this part of themselves, it will help them to overcome any stiffness that can attack either their minds or their bodies.

Men of this totem, like the bull elk, are competitive with each other about the women in their lives. They dislike ever terminating a relationship totally, preferring instead to keep all of their old lovers as good friends, a harem of sorts. Elk women, while not as showy as the men, are also competitive and like to keep all of their old men friends around, even if they are not actively relating to each other. While Elk people usually remain as rational as possible about this sort of competition, this is one of the areas in which they tend to not communicate their true feelings, which can sometimes lead them to unexpected fits of rage or jealousy.

Elk women make good mothers, taking the necessary time, when their babies are young, to give them a solid foundation of love and approval. As the children grow, they loosen the reins that they hold over them and usually relinquish them completely when the child is old enough to handle himself. Elk men are not usually enthusiastic about impending parenthood or infancy, but, as the child grows, they will delight in teaching him or her all that they can from what they have learned of life.

Elk children are quiet during their very early days, later developing into precocious learners capable of absorbing anything that they see or hear. They are thoughtful and considerate children, but they, too, can be given to fits of rage that will usually surprise anyone around who is used to the normally placid nature of the child.

When people from other totems travel through this one, they can learn more about their own introspective and clairvoyant talents, the regal part of their own nature and their ability to share wisely the lessons that their trip around the Medicine Wheel has taught them.

Elk people are compatible with others of the Thunderbird clan, those of the Red Hawk and Sturgeon, and with the members of the Butterfly clan, those of the Otter, Deer and Raven. They particularly complement Deer people.

THE POWERS
OF THE DIRECTIONS

Each of the four directions has special qualities and lessons to teach. As you travel the Medicine Wheel and stand in the moons of the different directions, it is important to open yourself to these lessons, for they are ones of spirit and of power. In the vision of the Medicine Wheel, each direction had a Spirit Keeper, a Spirit Being responsible for teaching earth's children the power of the direction.

Each direction is associated with a season of the year and a time of the day. Each has an animal totem and a color that represents its time and season. To the North is the Spirit Keeper the Chippewa people called Waboose; to the East is Wabun; to the South is Shawnodese; to the West is Mudjekeewis, Chief of the Spirit Keepers and Father of the Winds. Each Spirit Keeper is responsible for bringing one of the winds to the earth. Waboose brings the cold Northern winds of winter, which purify the earth with their intensity and force most of earth's children to spend part of their time just keeping warm, relaxing and renewing themselves. Wabun brings the warm East winds of the spring, which soothe us, tease us and force us to open ourselves to the illumination and wisdom that the spring brings to us. Shawnodese brings the hot Southern winds of summer, which make us open ourselves totally to the growth that these times can bring. Mudjekeewis brings the cool Western breezes of the autumn, which help us to go within ourselves and find our own strengths and weaknesses.

There are three moons governed by each of the Spirit Keepers, and the people of these moons share the qualities that each direction gives to them. These are the qualities that can help them to reach out to the world of spirit, to open themselves more fully to the powers of the universe.

To help in understanding and remembering the Spirit Keepers and their animals, this section begins with a story that tells how each animal became associated with its direction.

How Buffalo, Eagle, Coyote and Bear
Began to Help the Spirit Keepers

A long time ago when the animals could still talk to each other and to humans, and when the spirit teachers sometimes dwelled among humans, four of the mightiest of the animals had a disagreement. Each of these animals felt that they were the best of the animals and that they deserved to be the chief of all the other animals. This caused bad feelings in the animal council where the bear had always been the chief. He had this position because he was strong and had always made wise decisions for the brothers and sisters. While most of the animals felt that the bear deserved to remain the chief, others sided with one or another of the animals challenging him.

One of the challengers was the buffalo. The buffalo said, "I am the strongest and most powerful of the animals, and I give generously of myself to all of our brothers and sisters in the human as well as animal kingdoms. I deserve to be the chief because of my purity of purpose and my ability to renew all those who receive my gifts."

Another challenger was the eagle. The eagle said, "I fly higher than any of the rest of the winged creatures. I see more clearly. I fly closer to the Great Spirit than anyone else in this council. Because of my clarity and wisdom, I deserve to be the chief of this council."

The other one to challenge bear's right to be the chief of the council was the coyote. Coyote said, "I am the trickiest of all of the animals. I can survive anywhere. I have the ability to teach things to all of you whether or not you want to learn. Because of the growth I bring about, I deserve to be your chief."

Bear said, "I have great respect for my brothers who wish to be chief, but you have no reason to oust me. I have always served you well. I am strong, yet I am always gentle in my decisions. I always think long and hard before I decide what I should do about any question that faces us. I wish to continue to serve you as I have."

After the four powerful animals finished speaking, all of the other animals had their chance as the talking stick passed around the circle. When the stick came full circle back to the bear, it became clear that the animals were evenly divided about who should be the chief. No consensus was possible. Everyone there felt bad because it was the first time they had ever disagreed so greatly. No one knew what to do. All four animals were powerful and had medicine that qualified them to be the chief.

During the council the animals noticed that the winds were blowing strongly from all four directions. They seemed to be trying to tell the council something. But, since everyone was so caught up in trying to prove that he was right and his favorite should be the chief, no one was really listening.

Finally, as all of the animals sat in silence preparing for the talking stick to pass once again, one of the spirit teachers appeared in their midst. He appeared as a powerful man of middle age, and, as he came, the West Wind blew strongly.

"I am Mudjekeewis, the Spirit Keeper of the West. Where I walk the West Wind follows. Long ago, before any of you were born, it was decided that I would be the chief of the keepers of the directions. Like you, Eagle, Bear, Buffalo and Coyote, all four of us who now keep the directions were strong. We were children of the same mother, and we all had her strength and wisdom plus the separate wisdom of each of our fathers. But rather than fight about who was the strongest and thus break the law of unity, we decided with our mother's help to each take responsibility for one quarter of the Medicine Wheel so we could each use our separate strengths in the best possible way. By doing this we made the wheel strong in all directions, and we made ourselves stronger by having a definite direction for our strength to take. I was chosen by One Greater to be the chief because I always think before I act, so my strength is tempered by introspection.

"I am sent now by One Greater to intervene in this council. It is clear by listening to you speak that it would take many years to reach consensus. During this time the law of unity among the animals would be broken as the followers of one contender fought against the followers of another. This would cause unnecessary harm to all of you, and to your other relations on the earth. The Great Spirit does not want this to happen. So each of you four will now merge your power with the power of one of the directions. In this way your strengths, too, will help to make the wheel strong, and each of you will have a specific direction that you follow. Bear, you will merge with me, with the West, because, like me, you are strong and you think long before you speak. When you serve with me, your coat will be black, like the night, with silver hairs to honor the stars. You will remain as the chief of the animal council as I am chief of the council of the winds."

"Buffalo, you will merge with the power of Waboose, of the North, as you share the qualities of renewal and of purity. When you serve with Waboose, your coat will be white, the color of the snow. Eagle, you will merge with the power of Wabun, of the East. With your clear vision you will help to bring the awakening, wisdom and illumination. When you serve with her, you'll wear golden feathers, the color of the dawn. Coyote, you will merge with the power of the South, Shawnodese. With your ability to teach and survive, you will help to bring growth and trust into being. When you serve with him, your coat will be the color of the midday sun spotting the fertile earth.

"So, my honored friends, be happy now with the gifts of power the Great Spirit has given to each of you. Each of you will serve best in the direction that you have been given, and you can all now contribute to the harmony of the creation. It is good."

Waboose, Spirit Keeper of the North

The power of the North, of Waboose, is the power of renewal and of purity. The season of Waboose is the winter, when the earth is lying dormant, seemingly asleep. The daily time of Waboose is the night, when day creatures lie in sleep, the small death. In human life the time of Waboose is the older years, when hair becomes like snow, when bodies go slower and minds are purified—turning from thoughts of the earth to thoughts of the spirit.

But the dormancy is only external. What happens to the things of the earth in winter, when time seems frozen, when nothing seems to be growing? The seeds of one season lie in the earth, resting, being purified, gathering in the earth energy that will allow them to burst forth into new life when the warmth of the Father Sun returns from the South to warm the Earth Mother. While the earth sleeps at the surface, she is sending her deepest energy into all of her children. During their period of rest she is preparing them for the period of rapid growth to follow.

At night, when resting from the thoughts of the material world, many come closer to the spirit than they do during any of their waking hours. During sleep many learn lessons that they cannot or will not learn during the time when they are awake. As they die to the world that is usually around, to the world that absorbs with things of the outside, they are born to the world of the spirit, to the world always within.

In a similar manner, when people reach their older years they come to a period of relative rest when they can contemplate their lives and the lessons that they have learned, and can prepare for the rapid growth and learning that will take place when they change both worlds and form. In these years thoughts become more like dreams of youth. All of the lessons of spirit learned before come to waking consciousness, as people prepare for their own renewal.

The power of Waboose is a paradoxical power. It is new life cloaked in death, rapid growth cloaked in rest. It is the power of the ice-goddess with a warm heart beneath a frozen exterior. It is the power of new life beginning to throb through an apparently rotting seed. It is the power of snow bringing water to a dry and thirsting earth. It is the power of the ice breaking large rocks into small pebbles. It is the power of the cold wind making water into ice. It is the power of the trees covered with ice crystals, dancing in the North Wind. It is the power of the animals huddling together for warmth, hunting together for food.

For humans, the time of Waboose can be a trying time. For those who live in nature it is a time when the cold forces one to spend more time inside, in closer contact with the people you live with. It is a time of testing of relationships, as the enforced closeness causes people to see things they can either ignore or escape when the weather allows them to be more with the outdoors. It is a time when the forces of nature often cause plans to shift. It is a time, when the North Wind blows her coldest, that you feel the cold in the pit of your stomach and begin to wonder whether you will ever really be warm again. It is a time when nature throws you into yourself so that you have to explore territory that might otherwise be unfamiliar. While it is a time of external rest, the time of Waboose is a time of internal growth.

The animal that is tied to the essence of Waboose is the white buffalo. The buffalo, in the old days, was the animal that gave of itself so that the people could live. When the people needed meat, the buffalo gave its meat. When the people needed shelter, the buffalo gave its hide for clothes and tipis. The white buffalo was very rare and was considered to be a sacred messenger. It represented the spirit that gave totally of itself and its essence. It was the White Buffalo Woman who brought the sacred pipe to the people.

Like the spirit of Waboose, the white buffalo brought the renewal of both body and spirit and the purity of his presence to purify the thoughts of all who saw him. The color of Waboose is white. White is the color of purity, of balance, of life renewing itself. It is the sum of all the colors and represents evolution and perfection.

The moons of the North are the Earth Renewal Moon, the Rest and Cleansing Moon and the Big Winds Moon. People born under these moons and the people standing at these points will have the attributes of Waboose and will have to learn the lessons it is her medicine to teach—the lessons of patience, purity and renewal.

People of the moons associated with Waboose all have above-average abilities to understand the mystical realms and to learn to use the powers that these realms can give. They find it easy to be healers and to develop the other psychic powers.

They all share a need to ground themselves, to learn to be of the earth as well as the sky. They all need to learn to let their emotions flow freely so that they do not block them to the point where spiritual development is difficult.

They all like being around people, but usually prefer to keep relationships either on a superficial level or on a level where they are clearly the ones who have the power. They find it difficult to learn to trust others, although they don't find it hard to like others. They have the capacity to understand the power of rejuvenation but must constantly purify themselves to do so.

Wabun, Spirit Keeper of the East

The power of Wabun, of the East, is the power of illumination and wisdom. The season of Wabun is the spring, when the earth is awakening from the sleep of winter and the new life which has been preparing itself in the womb of the earth bursts forth. The daily time of Wabun is the dawn, when life awakens from the sleep of night. In human life the time of Wabun is youth, the time of awakening to things both within and outside, the time when people are capable of illuminating others by the purity of their energy.

In the spring everything is new and fresh. The earth comes alive in all directions. Plants break through the earth, covering the previously blank winter landscape with their brilliant displays of color. The rocks gleam with new light as the ice goes and their changed surfaces are exposed to the mild sun. The animals begin to give birth to their young and to scamper all over the countryside looking for the fresh plants of spring to feed them and help them to grow. The air is alive as the insect people hatch and begin to fly about their business, singing the songs that the Great Spirit has given them. With all of the new life upon her the Earth Mother is illuminated. All life shows the wisdom that allows it to continue.

So it is with each dawn when the sun climbs above the horizon, illuminating the landscape of whatever season it is. The sun causes all of the children of the earth to awaken; to get up to greet the new day with its fresh promise. The old ones say that the sun gives a special wisdom to those humans who get up to greet its first rays. At the dawning, it is the time to take the knowledge of the spirit received in sleep and turn it outward, to guide your steps through the new day that has come.

For humans, youth is the time when everything is fresh and new, when they can see the universe in a raindrop and spend hours looking at the beauty of a blade of grass. Watch an infant stare at a tree and you'll know some of the power of Wabun. Take a toddler for a walk through the woods and you'll see even more. The eyes of the young are not covered with the cynical blinders that make many miss the little beauties of life. Coming, as they do, from the infinite land of the stars, they still retain more of the wisdom that the Great Spirit imparts to all as they begin their journey on the Earth Mother. In their wisdom they don't know the limitations of time, they don't feel the threat of death. To them, each moment is as fresh as the first sunbeam touching a drop of dew. Youth is the time of experiencing everything as a first. It is the time of swimming in the stream of pure energy unhampered by the limitations of age, or of fears. It is the time when vision is expanded, like that of the eagle, when people see as if from a high place.

The power of Wabun is straightforward. It is the power of illumination possible for all of earth's children, if they do not block it from coming. It is the power of enlightenment that comes when we know our proper place in the universe, our unity with all of our relations and the love that has powered the Creation from its beginnings. It is the power of the morning glory opening its petals to the rays of the sun. It is the power of the mist rising from the river, revealing the clear water beneath. It is the power of the birds singing to the dawn. It is the power of the sun's first rays coming over the horizon.

The animal associated with the East is the eagle, the highest flying of the winged creatures. Because of his ability to fly so high, the eagle is as close to the sky realm of the spirit as any of the earth's children can be. For this reason the old ones always used the feathers of the eagle when they made prayers that they wished the Great Spirit to hear. They used eagle feathers in their prayer markers, and in their headdresses. They prayed that the eagle would help them send their prayers to the spirit. They prayed that the eagle would help them to see clearly, as he does, so they could have illumination and wisdom. The eagle of Wabun is the golden eagle, whose feathers are the color of the rising sun. The colors of Wabun are the red and gold of the rising sun. Red is the color of vital energy, and gold is the color of illumination, wisdom and enlightenment.

Those born under the moons of the East—the Budding Trees Moon, the Frogs Return Moon and the Cornplanting Moon— and those passing through these places as they travel around the wheel will have the strengths of Wabun, the power of the East.

The people of the moons of Wabun represent the fresh energy of the spring, which works miracles on the face of the earth. The people of these totems usually use their powers to work with things of the earth, rather than in the realms above. The earth is one of their proper places, and their energy is necessary to make changes on this planet.

However, these folks have the ability to reach to the realms beyond those of earth, in a natural and intuitive way, and to bring the lessons of these realms into the work that they are doing here. The people associated with Wabun have wisdom, and the possibility of bringing illumination and enlightenment to themselves and those they touch.

To work well with the other realms, they need to learn to control their vital energy, so that it does not overwhelm them or those around them. This can be a difficult lesson for them, since their energy is so vibrant that it sometimes tends to have a life of its own. When their energies are not controlled, they find it difficult to work with others. Their direct earth energy can seem so aggressive that it puts others into a defensive position. When this happens, it can block the exchange of human energies so necessary for the unfoldment of the people associated with Wabun.

Shawnodese, Spirit Keeper of the South

The power of Shawnodese, the Spirit Keeper of the South, is the power of growth and of trust. The season of Shawnodese is the summer, when all of the earth's children grow rapidly, coming to maturity, trusting in the wisdom of the earth that allows them to grow rapidly and mature properly. The time of day of Shawnodese is midday, when the warmth of the sun has helped the buds of dawn to open to the blossoms of the day. In human terms the time of Shawnodese is the time of adulthood, when both the internal and external seeds of youth begin to rapidly grow and blossom and particular purposes of life begin to become clear.

In the summertime the promises of the spring are fulfilled. The plants that began to bud come to full blossom and bear their fruit. The rocks that glistened with the new sun of spring glow as they take in the warmth of the summer sun. The young animals grow rapidly as they eat from the abundance of the plant kingdom. All things in nature grow in both body and mind, as they mature and take in the wisdom of the living, breathing earth.

At midday the lessons of the spirit received during sleep are put into action as people make plans and their direction for the day grows and takes shape. This is the time of reaching outward and growing in the things of the world. It is the time of testing wisdom by bringing it into physical being and helping it to grow. Sometimes the original direction is correct, and sometimes it must change; to know, the idea must first become an external reality.

In human life young adult years are those of testing and searching. They are the years when people try all of the many things that seem to be their calling, when they experiment with the ideas that came to them in their youth. These are the years when people try growing in all of the directions that seem possible to them, gradually putting aside those that feel less than right. These are the magic years when nothing seems irreversible, when even mistakes are beneficial as long as they are the result of a sincere effort. These are the years that test and mold, preparing people to be strong in those things that they were born to do.

The power of Shawnodese is neither as paradoxical as the power of Waboose nor as straightforward as the power of Wabun.

It is the power of growing rapidly while learning to trust feelings and intuitions. It is the power of maturing. It is the power of the corn trusting that its early growth brought enough wisdom from the earth, that it cross-pollinated with the correct species to bring forth good, healthy kernels that will be of help to all who partake of it. It is the power that brings humans together to form new life, which they, too, hope will be healthy, happy and able to bring joy. It is the power that directs the corn pollen to the proper silk and directs the man or woman to the proper mate. It is the primal power that guides all of the earth's children to mate so that the growth they have experienced can continue even when their season of rapid growth has passed.

The animal that is associated with Shawnodese is the coyote. To Native people the coyote is the trickster, the one who can force folks to learn even when they don't want to. By his tricks coyote forces his relations to grow. By being tricked and then learning necessary lessons, earth's children learn to trust in life and in the lessons that it brings. Being as stubborn as most of earth's children are, tricks are often necessary to growth. People become comfortable as they are and don't wish to experience the pain that rapid growth sometimes brings. At such times the power of Shawnodese and the coyote is needed to help people grow and continue to learn the lessons that they were placed on earth to learn. The coyote of Shawnodese has a yellow coat, the color of the midday sun, mottled with the brown of the summer earth.

The colors of Shawnodese are the green of the plants rapidly growing and the yellow of the summer sun giving them the heat and light so they can grow. Green is the color of growth, trust, healing and restoring energy and yellow is the color of intelligence, mental receptivity and natural wisdom.

Those born under the moons of Shawnodese—the Strong Sun Moon, the Ripe Berries Moon and the Harvest Moon—and those who are passing through the stages of these moons on their trip around the wheel, will experience rapid growth and all of the lessons that this will bring to them.

The people of the moons of Shawnodese are ones with the capacity for rapid growth, on all levels, once they have firmly put their foundations into the earth. These folks must have their earth energies firmly grounded and connected with a good direction before they are able to reach out for things of the spirit.

The people of Shawnodese must learn to trust their intuition while they are dealing with the energies of the earth. It is this that will direct them to the places where they can apply their energy and their power. They must allow their intuition to help them to mature so that they will be able to follow the path that they should. They must bear their fruit on the earth, before they can allow their energies to reach out to the things beyond the earth. If they don't, they risk misusing their spiritual energies by applying them to earth things for personal gains. Such use will keep them from being able to develop further.

People of these moons are loving, friendly, gregarious folks who usually touch many others with their energies, their knowledge and their love. As long as this touching comes from the good energy of their hearts, it will bring good to them and those around them.

Mudjekeewis, Spirit Keeper of the West

The power of Mudjekeewis, Spirit Keeper of the West, is the power of strength and introspection. The season of Mudjekeewis is the autumn, when the growth of summer stops and earth's children prepare for their season of renewal. The daily time of Mudjekeewis is the sunset and twilight, when the activity of the day slows down and day's creatures prepare for their time of sleep and renewal. In human life the time of Mudjekeewis is the middle years, when people have found their direction and work strongly to achieve those tasks that they have been given for this lifetime.

While the time of Mudjekeewis is a slower time than that of Shawnodese, it is a stronger time. Plants come to their full maturity as their blossoms become the seeds for plants to come. Rocks lose the warmth of the summer sun but strengthen their internal structure so they don't crumble during the first frost. The ones newly born in the previous spring strengthen their bodies for the winter to come. All of the things in nature stop their growing and consolidate the growth that they have had, the things that they have learned in the previous season. They begin to look within themselves and see what is strong enough to survive the time of renewal that is to come.

As the sun sets in the West, humans, too, stop their outward activities and take time to contemplate what gains they have made, what lessons they have learned. In the semilight of dusk thoughts begin to turn from things of the world to things of the spirit. This is the time to evaluate the gains or losses of the day, so minds are clear to learn the lessons that come in sleep.

In human life the middle years are those of power. You have experienced some of life. You have learned some of its lessons and made your initial mistakes. You have tried working on the many projects that seemed appealing in your youth and often have found the direction that you were meant to take. Once you find your direction, you receive the power that comes with knowing where you are going. You are no longer subject to change at every hint of a new idea, nor dazzled by every strong personality that you meet. You know the path that you are walking, and you are able to walk it in a calm and peaceful manner. The middle years are the ones of responsibility. There are growing children to raise, there are aging parents to care for, there are younger brothers and sisters to teach and help to find their own paths. You must be strong to be able to follow your direction while doing all of these other things. You must have spent much time looking within so that you know your own strengths and weaknesses and can work with others without thinking that their weaknesses are your own.

In its own way the power of Mudjekeewis is as straightforward as the power of Wabun. It is the power of strength that can come only from knowing yourself. It is the power of the spirit coming to the earth. It is the power that comes from the ability and freedom to be idealistic and selfless serving the world in all ways possible to you. It is the power of a stable mineral, a matured plant, animal or human who is well on the way to fulfilling its reason for existence. It is the power of the twilight changing the landscape of the earth. It is the power of the nighthawks circling and singing to the earth. It is the power of the sunset throwing its color over the earth. It is the power of the moon as she begins to rise.

The animal of Mudjekeewis is the grizzly bear, the strongest of the bears. The grizzly is able to live by its own strength. It knows the ways of life and the ways of the earth well enough to heal itself of most illnesses. Like all bears, it is able to make the great sleep in winter, awaken renewed and then find the herbs and mud that will give it the energy to be ready for the springtime. The fall is its time of preparation, when the bear readies itself for the time of renewal to come by eating well and strengthening its body. The bear is considered to be the chief of the council of the animals because, with all its strength the bear is gentle and is introspective about all decisions that he must make. Because the bear has looked within himself and knows his own heart, he is able to look within the hearts of the other animals and help them to learn the lessons that they must. The grizzly of Mudjekeewis is black like the night, with some silver hairs. The colors of Mudjekeewis are the blues of twilight merging into the blacks of night. Blue is the color of spiritual strength, idealism and selflessness. Black is the color of one looking within and purposely blinding oneself to the things of the earth, of the formlessness from which all things can come.

Those born under the moons of Mudjekeewis—the Ducks Fly

Moon, the Freeze Up Moon and the Long Snows Moon—and those who travel through their times of being governed by these moons will have to learn to look within and find their own strengths and weaknesses.

The people of the moons of Mudjekeewis represent the strength and the power that come to the earth in autumn, the season of looking within. They have the strength that only comes to those who have looked within themselves and truly evaluated the things that they found. They are the people who know their place on the earth and are able to reach out to other realms with the power that this knowledge gives to them.

People born under the moons of this direction are comfortable both with the things of the earth and with those of the spirit. They have the patience necessary to journey between these realms. They have the ability to be leaders and teachers in either of these spheres, as long as they have learned to control the confusion that their own power and adaptability can bring to them. The moons of Mudjekeewis, the Chief of the Spirit Keepers, are moons of power, and this power can affect those born under them in either positive or negative ways, depending upon their willingness to truly know themselves, their own gifts and liabilities.

People of this direction are powerful and will affect many others. Whether their effect promotes unity or disharmony depends upon their individual honesty and strength.

THE ELEMENTAL CLANS

The elemental clan under which you were born tells you which of the elements you most easily relate to and which element you have a particular responsibility for. It tells you of the characteristics you share with your clan relations— strengths and weaknesses that you have in common.

There are four of these clans, as there are four basic elements from which the earth is built. These are the earth, the water, the air and the fire. Without these elements, life would not have begun and could not continue. The earth with all her minerals is the basic building block of life as we know it. The Earth Mother gives the stable base upon which the lives of all her children are built. The Earth Mother, from her generous and patient center, nourishes and sustains, allowing all life to grow.

Without water, nothing else could exist. Even the earth would dry, crumble and blow away. Without water's constantly flowing movement, the earth would not change and shift, the air would be arid and the fire would burn out of control. Earth's children would eventually dry up and die without the special nourishment that comes only from water.

Most of earth's children need the air to breathe so their lives can continue. Humans, the plants and the animals all need elements of the air for our life processes to work. The water needs the air to carry it from one location to another, and our Earth Mother needs the winds the air brings to keep her stability from becoming static. The sun needs the air to carry his rays to the earth, and the fire needs air to begin and continue.

Without the fire of the sun shining upon the earth, life would end. It is the marriage of the energies of the Father Sun and Earth Mother that causes new life to begin and continue. Without fire, water would freeze, and air would chill. Plants, animals and humans would not have the warmth or the light that they need to live.

How connected each element is to the others, and how connected people are to each of them, and to all their relations! In the sweat lodge, after remembering each element, the old ones asked to feel the connection, the unity between them all. The steam caused by pouring water on the rocks taken from the fire fills the air, and they felt that unity within and around.

All of the elements are very necessary to life, yet many tend to forget their connection to them, their responsibility to be thankful for the gifts that they bring. By learning, first, of your beginning element, you can start to feel that connection and see your responsibility. By studying the people of the elements with which you can combine, or be complementary, you can learn more. Remember that these complements and combinations apply as much to friends and associates as to spouses or lovers. As you travel around the Medicine Wheel, your knowledge will grow. People of the different elemental clans are as connected and needful of each other as their elements. Through combining energies, everyone can learn, grow and change.

Preceding each clan section is a story about the totem animal of the clan. These stories will help you to remember things you might otherwise forget.

How Turtle Helped to Build Our Land

A long time ago the Great Spirit looked upon the earth he had created according to his vision, and he became sad. The minerals, the plants, the animals and the humans had all forgotten the law of unity by which they were to live. They were fighting with each other over the smallest idea or action. They were being possessive of the powers and talents they had been given. They were showing jealousy, hatred, greed. The Great Spirit decided that the earth could not continue in this way. He tried to send messages to all of earth's children to tell them to live in a better way, but only some of the minerals, plants and animals would listen. The humans acted deaf. So he decided to send all those who didn't listen into different realms where they could hear him and learn their lessons. He called all the spirits of water together and they descended upon the earth. The rain came and rained streams all over the earth. The waves rose up and covered all of the land. Only the minerals and a few plants and animals survived. Still, the Great Spirit felt sad, for an earth without humans was not an earth that would fulfill the vision that he had been given.

Up in the clouds there lived a spirit woman who, at one time, had lived upon the earth. With most of the life gone from the earth there wasn't anything for her to watch or help with and she became lonely. She asked the Great Spirit to send her a spirit man. One came and, eventually, they mated and she became pregnant. The spirit man left then as he had fulfilled his purpose. She was again alone in the skies.

The animals on earth were lonely, too, for companionship similar to that the humans had given them in earlier days when they remembered the law of unity. They saw the woman in the sky and decided to invite her to come to the earth. But they were perplexed because they knew that she would need land to walk upon, and everything was then under the water. While they sat in council on some rocks that protruded above the waters wondering what to do, the giant turtle came and stuck his head out of the water.

"Friends," Turtle said, "I have a large, strong back. Perhaps the Sky Woman would come here if I rose my back out of the water so that she could come and be on it."

"Wonderful," said Bear, chief of the council. "That would be the perfect solution. We will ask her to come be with us and have her children here so that they can grow up among us and learn young the harmony in which we should live. And perhaps they will teach this to their children."

So the animals had Turtle raise his back up out of the water and they all crawled from their various rocks onto it. They ran around and bounced and jumped and played because they were happy to have a large space to walk upon again, and they also wanted to make sure all the movement wouldn't hurt Turtle. They knew how much more movement humans would make. When they were satisfied that his was a good home, they called up to Sky Woman and asked her to come down and be among them. She accepted, happy that she would not have to be lonely anymore.

When she came down, she walked all around the turtle's back and saw that it was indeed a large and fine home. This took her many days to do because the turtle was a very large one. When she came back to the eastern place where she began, she said, "Turtle, you are a brave and strong animal to offer your back to me and to all of the humans that will come from me and my children. If you stay as our home forever, you will not have the chance to do the things that turtles should, so I will help you. Water animals, go and search out the land at the bottom of the ocean and bring some back to me."

All of the water animals dove down and tried. Some brought back a grain of earth but there wasn't enough. Finally, when they had all just about given up, the muskrat came up with a mouthful of dirt and laid it at the Sky Woman's feet before collapsing. After she used her medicine to revive Muskrat, she took tne eartn and again walked all around Turtle's back. As she walked, she dropped the earth all around the back. When she got back to the beginning, she breathed the breath of life upon the earth and it multiplied, covering all of Turtle's back.

"Turtle," said Sky Woman, "you may now return to your life. But, in honor of the sacrifice that you made and were ready to make, this land shall be called Turtle Island, and even though you tend to be a creature of the water you will also be thought of as the creature of this land, this part of the earth."

And that is how Turtle became the totem of the earth clan.

Turtle Clan • Earth

Those who belong to the Turtle elemental clan have the stability that comes from association with the first and most stable of elements, the earth. They are rooted in the element that sustains all of us from the time we are born. Like the earth, they tend to sustain all those with whom they come in contact. When they settle in a location or situation, they immediately send their roots down and provide a stable base upon which to build.

Turtle clan people tend to be the foundation stones of their family, their business, their friends. They are very loyal. Once they have decided that something is right for them, they find it very difficult to change their minds. They are constant in their opinions, ideals and ideas. Because of this trait, they can be both a great source of security and one of frustration to those who know them. If you have friends in the Turtle clan, you can depend upon them to remain your friends, unless you do something that conflicts with an ideal that they cherish more than your friendship. But woe upon you if you tell a Turtle friend that you'll do something with him and then, for any reason, change your mind. Because Turtle clan people keep their word through just about anything, they don't understand others who do not do the same.

This is not to say that Turtle clan people all become as hard as rocks in all of their ways. Some do, and that is one of the things that those of this clan must guard against. Others, however, like the earth, embody the concept of growth as well as stability. Turtle clan people, once they are rooted, will help their friends, their businesses and their ideas to grow. The growth that they bring about is solid, constructive, channeled growth. They take one step at a time, rather than rapidly racing forth in a burst of intuition. Like the earth, they want the seedling of change to sprout before it grows, flowers and bears seeds. Because of their slow growth, changes that they make tend to be permanent ones and, usually, constructive ones. If you are beginning any new project, try to include at least one person of the Turtle clan to make sure that the project progresses as well as it possibly can.

Members of the Turtle clan, like their totem, sometimes appear

---

slow, even clumsy, but this is often just the outward appearance. Like the turtle, they are intelligent and crafty, and most often win the race with whatever hare they are racing. Turtle clan people usually attain any goals that they seek simply because they keep on trying long after their competitors have given up.

Turtle clan people, like the earth, make good parents. But they can have some fixed ideas about how to bring their children up. They worry, frequently unnecessarily, over situations over which they seem to have no control. As parents they are protective and methodical. They don't understand when their children act in an unpredictable way, and they will often try to push children into the pattern that they, not the children, are comfortable with. They really love their children and will always be there when their children need them, no matter what age the children have attained. They have to be careful to not attempt to totally run their children's lives for them.

Turtle clan children may appear to start out slower than others in their age group, but soon, through their tenacity, they will catch up to or go beyond those they lagged behind. They are children who need schedules and set rules of conduct to be happy. Given these, they are very stable, intelligent and happy little people.

Like the turtle in the story about this clan, Turtle clan folks tend to be self-sacrificing. If they see a place where they can be of great service, they will strive to fill it, even if this means giving up the things that they are supposed to be doing in life. Because of their bravery and stubbornness, they find it difficult to extricate themselves from situations that prove untenable. Sometimes this can lead them to become martyrs to a cause or person that they should have left long ago.

Because Turtle clan people represent the earth, they have a responsibility to her. They generally feel a great resonance with nature and are not comfortable if they do not have the opportunity to go to natural places frequently. Being in such places restores and revitalizes their spirits, and Turtle clan people always look younger and happier after such jaunts. Of course, Turtle people make marvelous gardeners, and they love to surround themselves with plants. If they have land, you will always be able to tell which gardens are theirs, because theirs will be lush and beautiful.

If they live in the cities, you will feel as though you are going into a jungle when you enter their homes because of the gorgeous plants that will surround you. Those who are in a Turtle clan position or mood will always have greener thumbs than they ever did in any other periods of their lives. In fact, to become a good gardener, you have to have passed through at least one of the Turtle clan signs.

Turtle clan people have a responsibility to the Earth Mother. Since they are of her, they must remember her. They must take the time to look at the earth, with appreciation. When they become comfortable doing so, they must remember to thank the earth, in their hearts, for all of the wonderful sustenance she gives them and all of their relations. Turtle clan people are also connected to the rocks, and they should take time to admire rock formations that they see, and to be thankful that they are there. They should also bring some of the rocks that particularly attract them into their homes, as this will make them feel more comfortable and more connected with all of the universe. Turtle clan people will find that these rocks can speak to them if they take the time to listen.

One message that the rocks may give them is to be cautious that they don't become too much like them. That is perhaps the greatest potential pitfall for those of the Turtle clan: to become crystallized, stubborn and inflexible. When this happens, those of the Turtle clan effectively close themselves off from the flow of life, and they stop the energy of growth that also flows through them. If this happens, Turtle clan people are prone to the illnesses of physical stiffness: arthritis, rheumatism, chronic back pain and other maladies that come from stiff muscles or bones.

Snow Goose, Beaver and Brown Bear people are those born under the Turtle clan. Because of this, these folks will always have a great attraction to the earth, no matter where they are standing on the wheel. To be happy and fulfilled in their lives they will have to learn to admit this attraction and to live their lives in such a way that they will always have some closeness to the earth. Those born under other totems will pass through Turtle clan signs as they travel around the wheel and, during these times, they will experience the stability, tenacity and sustaining nature of those born under the Turtle clan.

Why Some Frogs Left the Water

A long time ago the frogs lived in all of the ponds, lakes and rivers of the world, in the same way that many of them do today. They were happy singing their songs, sitting on their lily pads and laying the eggs that become pollywogs and then, as if by magic, become frogs. It was a good life, and most of the frogs were happy.

Then, one day, one of the chiefs of the frogs, whose name was Ripid-do, became dissatisfied. Every day, from his lily pad, he could see something in the distance. This thing that he saw was large, larger than anything he had ever seen before. It was green most of the way up, and then it became white. As he would watch, many of the other animals would go up there, looking hungry, and, hours later, they would return, looking as though they had had a lot to eat. He began to be dissatisfied with the flies, mosquitoes and water bugs that he usually ate.

"On this large thing," he thought, "there must be delicious things to eat. That is why all of the other animals look so full and happy when they come down from it. It isn't fair that we frogs have to stay in this pond always eating the same old things. I want to go to this big thing and get some of the good things that they always have to eat."

One day he called to a snake that he saw slithering down the large thing and asked him where he had been and what he had had to eat.

"That large thing," said the snake, "is a mountain. Up on it are the biggest, juiciest, most delicious bugs that I have ever eaten. They make the biggest flies here seem like gnats. Um, how happy I am that I can go to the mountain."

Ripid-do thought about what the snake said, and he became terribly hungry for the delicacies that the snake described. He began to tell all of the other frogs about them. He made them sound so good that all of the frogs wanted to have a chance to have some of them to eat. Soon the frogs in that pond told the frogs in the next pond about them, and so it spread until all of the frogs in all of the ponds, streams, lakes and rivers all around the mountain became dissatisfied with what the Great Spirit had given them.

Finally, Ripid-do made a bold suggestion.

"Fellow frogs," he proposed, "since the Great Spirit is trying to keep us from all that is best in life for us, let us set out on our own and climb that mountain and forget about the places where we live now."

Some of the frogs agreed. They had really come to believe that they were being forgotten or ignored by the Great Spirit. Others felt that, although those other bugs might be bigger, it would be difficult for them to live on a mountain, out of water.

"You are cowards," Ripid-do told these frogs. "We frogs can live on land. We can do anything. Don't we sit all day on lily pads out of the water? The Great Spirit just told us that we have to be in water to keep us from all of the best things that all of the other animals have. Let us set off for the mountain."

After he finished his speech, and while it was being broadcast to all of the other frogs in all of the other ponds, Ripid-do heard a voice in his mind.

"Little brother," said the voice, "I have given you all that you need to live well. Don't be greedy for things that other animals have. Be happy and sing your songs of thanks for the good things that you have. And don't go to the mountain today. Things will not go well for you if you do."

Although this made Ripid-do hesitate, he was so determined that he was missing out on something that he ignored the warning of the Great Spirit. Soon he and the frogs who followed him set off for the mountain. As they started their climb up it, they noticed that all of the other animals who usually went up there to feed were busy running down.

"Things aren't right on the mountain today," the snake he had spoken to before told him. "Go back to your ponds."

The frogs were determined. Ripid-do felt that the Great Spirit had told all of the other animals to act in this way to trick the frogs, and that the animals had agreed because they didn't want to share all of the food they had with the army of frogs marching up the mountain.

Up they went, looking for the delicious bugs they thought they would find. In fact, some of the frogs did find a few bugs and they were the biggest that they had ever seen and the most delicious. But most of the insects, too, were flying in large swarms down from the mountain.

As they continued up they noticed that the white snow from

the top of the mountain was melting and torrents of water were beginning to run down the mountain. Some of the frogs became scared when they saw this and wanted to turn back. But Ripid-do called them cowards and challenged them to continue. Soon the torrents of water were joined by melted rock running down the side of the mountain, and a large cloud of steam began to envelop all of the frogs, causing their skins to burn.

"Don't turn back now, brothers and sisters," shouted Ripid-do. "If we show the Great Spirit that we won't fall for his tricks, all of this will soon disappear."

It didn't. It became worse as the volcano continued to erupt. Ripid-do wasn't sure what to do. He realized, at the last minute, that he had brought many of his brothers and sisters into danger simply because he felt what he wanted was more important than what the Great Spirit had given him.

"Great Spirit," he prayed with all his might, "I will sacrifice myself gladly if you will somehow save all of the frogs following me. It isn't fair that they suffer for my mistake. I should have listened to your warning and the warnings of the other animals."

"Little brother," he heard a voice say in his ear, "I will save all who follow you, as they now have learned their lesson. Have them hop into the waterfall that you see up ahead. It will safely carry them back into their ponds, streams and rivers. But don't you hop into it yourself."

Ripid-do did as he was told. Soon all of the other frogs were being carried by the water to safety.

Ripid-do sat there as the steam thickened. He was awaiting his fate, knowing that he had done wrong. Suddenly a burst of wind came and blew him into a tree that was so high on the mountain the steam didn't reach it. He was safe and watched as the volcano finished its eruption.

"Little brother," he heard the voice again, "since you so much wanted to live on the mountain, this is where you'll be from now on. You'll be smaller than you were before, and you'll no longer live in the water. The trees will be your home and the home of your children for all generations to come."

So the tree frogs, that strange, land-borne relative of the water-happy frogs, came to be.

Frog Clan ▪ Water

The people who belong to the Frog elemental clan have the qualities associated with that most flowing, changing and renewing element. Without water, most life would cease. Without water, earth's children would never be cleansed in their physical and emotional beings. The action of the water can remove blockages wherever they occur. Watch a stream that comes in contact with rocks that would keep it from flowing. Soon the water will seep under or splash over. Eventually, the power of its flowing moves the rocks and makes a channel through which it can freely run.

So it is with people of the Frog clan. Their emotions, like the water, are constantly flowing. They feel in their hearts all of the things within themselves and around them. They are the ones who mutter "Ouch" when someone else hits his thumb with a hammer. They are the ones who gasp when they see a running child fall. They are the ones who share your tears of happiness and of sadness.

Frog clan people feel, and feel deeply. Because of this, they are capable of empathizing with others, no matter what they are feeling. Like the water, they sometimes provide clear reflections to other people of just what they are like at any given moment. Since they are connected to the water, which is connected strongly to the power of the moon, Frog clan people tend more than others to be governed by the moon and its phases. When the moon is full, they are like the tide, rippling with emotions or crashing into the rocks. At these times, they do not provide a clear reflection for those around them. When the moon is dark, they, like the water, are calmer, and they provide a still surface for reflection.

Because of their ability to feel, Frog clan people can bring new feelings, new life, into any project. Since they can flow so easily, they can clean out the mental and physical cobwebs that they find in any place that they go. Frog clan people are good to have involved in a project of any kind when it seems that it just can't go any further. It is at these times that Frog people can find the crack they can seep under, breaking loose the obstructions that were stopping the progress. Frog clan people don't tend to do things halfway, so when they break an obstruction loose, it really comes loose.

As parents Frog clan people give their children constantly flowing love. They are very nurturing, because they are so close to their emotions. However, they sometimes tend to try to round off the rough edges they think they see on their children before they have given the children the chance to develop enough to see if the edge is really the cornerstone for their next period of growth. They feel so deeply they will also sometimes be overly protective, since any pain that their children feel tends to hurt them. They must be careful to let their children experience their own lives, rather than trying to shield them from all experiences that could cause them any pain.

Frog clan children are very emotional and empathetic. Until they have grown enough to understand their empathy, they need protection or they will always be getting sick when anyone else is ill, or failing subjects their best friends just can't understand. Given protection and direction until they can understand all the emotions they feel, they are very loving and joyful folks.

Water is an element of healing. Because of their association with water, Frog clan people often have a natural gift for healing, whether of the body or the emotions. Remember, it is often an emotional blockage that brings about a physical disorder. Frog clan people can help you to locate the blockages within yourself, and, if you let them, they will direct their flowing energy toward these blockages in such a way that they will begin to dissolve. In many cases being able to let your own water flow, in the form of tears, is the first step toward being healed of whatever is troubling you. The Frog clan friends you have are the ones to turn to at such times.

Because they are constantly swimming in the sea of energy around all of us, Frog clan people tend to be very creative. Whether they work in the arts or in other fields, they will come up with the fresh, new ideas that spark a revolution in whatever field they are in. Of course, as soon as the idea becomes a trend, the Frog clan people are swimming off to seek something that seems newer and fresher.

Like Ripid-do, the lead frog in the Frog clan story, water clan people always have their ears open for things that are newer and better. They are always ready to float downstream to try these new things out. If they can't get to them, they, like Ripid-do, often feel dissatisfied, and they really begin to yearn for those things that they can't have.

It is at those points that Frog clan people have to be cautious. If they fixate on something that seems difficult to obtain, they stop themselves from flowing with the energy of life, and they begin to block themselves up. When this happens, they hold back all the magnificent energy that usually flows around them. After a time, they feel like dams that are about to burst.

This will sometimes happen to Frog clan people when they become afraid at the depths of the feelings that they have, and they begin to hold back their emotions. They try to convince themselves and those around them that they are unfeeling. While this charade goes on, their emotions are gathering more and more power. The more force their emotions get, the more afraid they are to let them loose.

Sometimes Frog clan people go through life in this manner, always holding back and repressing the emotions and energy that they feel both within and around them. When they do this, they will tend toward the illnesses that cause the body to seem lumpy or bloated—obesity, edema, deformations of the bones or muscles. In their minds they will seem frozen, like water that has turned to ice. The basic cure for this is for the Frog clan people to find a way to let their water, their energy, begin to seep through, so the dams they have created won't burst and the water come rushing out in a way that will hurt them or those around them.

Frog clan people are refreshed by being around water, whether it is the sea, a lake, pond, river, or water in a tub. Frog clan children can often be calmed from the most ferocious temper tantrum by letting them hear the sound of running water. Because of their clan, these people have a responsibility to the water, to appreciating and encouraging it to flow cleanly and properly. This is a particularly important responsibility in these times when we have polluted so much of the water that we use and when we show so little appreciation for the gift of water. Say "thanks" next time it rains, not "darn, there go my plans for the day." Write your radio and television weathermen and tell them that it can be a beautiful day when it's raining, too.

Frog clan people also have a responsibility to the moon, which helps to govern human emotions. They should get to know the moon and the secrets that she holds for humankind. They should also get to know their own emotions and how to keep them flowing constructively. When they know this, they can help others who have blocked their own from flowing.

Cougar, Flicker and Snake people are those born under the clan of the water, with the totem of the frog. To be happy in their lives they have to be certain that they allow themselves always to be in the liquid flow of the universal energies. They need to learn to appreciate the water that is within them and around them. Those born under other elemental clans will experience the empathy, creativity and healing energy of those of the Frog clan as they travel to their places on their journey around the wheel.

How Butterflies Learned to Fly

When the earth was young, there were no butterflies to fly by and brighten the spring and summer days with their wings carrying some of the colors of the rainbow. There were crawlers who were the ancestors of butterflies, but they didn't know how to fly and they would just crawl along the earth. These crawlers were beautiful to see, but all too often people wouldn't watch the earth as they walked and so they missed observing their beauty.

In these days, there was a young woman named Spring Flower, and she was a delight to all who knew her. She always had a smile and a kind word, and her hands felt like the coldest spring to those who were sick with fevers or burns. She would lay her hands upon them, and the fever would leave their body. When she reached the time of womanhood, her power became even stronger, and, after her vision, she was capable of healing people from most of the sicknesses they could have in those days.

In her vision strange and beautiful flying creatures had come to her and given her the power of the rainbow that they carried with them. Each color of the rainbow had a special quality of healing that these flyers revealed to her. They told her that, during her life, she would be able to heal, and, at the time of her death, she would release healing powers into the air that would stay with the people for all times. The name given to her in her vision was She Who Weaves Rainbows in the Air.

As She Who Weaves Rainbows in the Air grew older, she continued her healing work and her kindness to all whom she met. She also met a man, a dreamer, and took him as her husband. They had two children together and raised them to be strong, healthy and happy. The two children also had some of the powers of their parents and, later in life, became healers and dreamers themselves.

As She Who Weaves Rainbows in the Air became older, her power increased even more, and people from all around the area where she lived came to her with their sick ones, asking her to try to heal them. Those that she could help she helped.

Eventually, the effort of letting all the power come through her made her tired, and she knew that the time to fulfill the other part of her vision drew near. During her life she had noticed that beautifully colored crawlers always came near to her when she sat on the earth. They would come close to her hand and try to rub themselves against it. Sometimes one would crawl up her arm and perch near her ear.

One day when she was resting such a crawler came by her ear. She spoke to it, asking it to tell her what she could do to be of service, as she noticed that it and its brothers and sisters had always been of service to her.

"Sister," said the crawling one, "my people have always been there when you have been healing, helping to bring the colors of the rainbow to you through the colors we wear on our bodies. Now that you are passing into the world of spirit, we don't know how we can continue to bring the healing of these colors to the people. We are earthbound, and the people rarely look down so that they can see us. We feel that if we could fly, the people would notice us and smile at the beautiful colors they see. And we could fly around those who need healing and let the powers of our colors give them whatever healing they can accept. Can you help us to fly?"

She Who Weaves Rainbows in the Air promised to try. She told her husband of her conversation and asked him if any messages might come to him in his dreams.

The next morning he woke up, excited, from the dream he had had. When he gently touched She Who Weaves Rainbows in the Air to tell her of it, she did not respond. He sat up and looked closely and saw that his wife had passed into the spirit world during that night.

Through the time of praying for her soul and making preparations for the burial, he remembered that dream that he had had. It comforted him. When it was time to take She Who Weaves Rainbows in the Air to the grove where she would be buried, he looked on her bedding, and waiting for him was the crawler he had expected to find. He gently lifted it up and took it with him.

As they put his wife's body into the earth and prepared to place the soil over her, he heard the crawler say, "Put me on her shoulder now. When the earth is over us, my body, too, will die, but my spirit will merge with the spirit of the one who was your wife and together we will fly out of the earth. Then we will go back to my people and teach them how to fly so that the work your wife began can continue. She is waiting for me to come. Put me there now."

The man did as the crawler told him to do, and the burial proceeded. When all of the others had left, the man stayed behind for a while. He looked at the grave, remembering all the love he had had. Suddenly from the grave came a flying one with all the colors of the rainbow spread over its wings. It flew to him and landed on his shoulder.

"Do not be sad, my husband. Now my vision is totally fulfilled, and those who I'll help to teach now will always bring goodness, healing and happiness to the people. When your time comes to pass into spirit, I'll be waiting to rejoin you."

When the man did change worlds, several years later, and was buried, his children stayed behind after all of the others had gone. They noticed a beautiful one of the new creatures they called butterflies hovering near the grave. In a few minutes another butterfly of equal beauty flew up out of their father's grave and joined the one who was waiting and, together, they flew to the North, the place of renewal.

From that time on butterflies have always been with the people brightening the air, and our lives, with their beauty.

Butterfly Clan • Air

Those who are associated with the element of air, who have the butterfly as the totem of their clan, are always changing and shifting, like the air around us. Like the air, they have the power of transforming the things and the people that they touch. While their energy is one of constant change, like that of the water, the changes that they bring can often be sudden, rather than gradual. They can shift things around like a strong gust of wind blowing from an unexpected direction.

Butterfly clan people are always in motion, physically, mentally and emotionally. The energy of life blows through them, bringing them new ideas, new feelings, new thoughts. Sometimes it is difficult for them to catch on to any one of these things, as their energy is so rapid and, sometimes, so unexpected.

While water heals, rejuvenates and refreshes, air transforms. Look out your window and door one day when one of the winds is blowing, and see how different everything looks. The trees, usually calm and stately, are suddenly playful creatures dancing in the sun or moonlight. Meadows of grass look like rippling seas as the wind parts them first in one direction, then in another. Fields of dandelions are lifted into the air and their seeds deposited where they will best reproduce in the year to come. Humans look different, too, as the wind sweeps their hair back, rearranges their clothes and causes their faces to look stronger and more determined.

Those of the Butterfly clan are like the air. When they come into a room, a project or a business, they transform the details and, sometimes, uproot the very foundations. Butterfly clan people have an active energy. When they see the need for a change, they want that change to happen today, not next week. They often tend to be manipulative, to make sure that the changes they feel need to happen occur sooner, not later. But, even in their manipulation, they have the purity of the wind, as long as their energy is flowing properly.

Like the air, Butterfly clan people contain the breath of life. This is the force that enables them to transform things with which they are involved. Because they contain this breath of life, they are always full of new plans and ideas, and all of them seem absolutely essential to them. They live life fully, sometimes too much so. They have to be cautious not to overextend themselves and try to accomplish more than it is possible for one person to do.

Butterfly clan people, like the butterfly in the legend about this clan, are always looking for ways in which to serve their people. They are happiest when they are in a position that allows them to shift and change, while still serving their fellow humans. They also enjoy being of service to their relations in the mineral, plant and animal kingdoms. You will often find Butterfly clan people in the positions of service: healers of mind, spirit or body.

Butterfly clan people literally bring a breath of fresh air into anything in which they are involved. They are intelligent and creative, and they are quick to see where the weak points of any plan are. They are as quick to see them as they are to point them out, though they will often do so in such a pleasing way that you won't even known that you are being corrected. Most often these people have the gentleness of the East or South winds, or the sultry spirit of the night wind blowing through the forest. While things around them are always in motion, the motion is usually gentle enough that it is sometimes hard to recognize. This constant motion does not make Butterfly people the world's best organizers.

When a Butterfly clan person is crossed, you can encounter anything from the strong West Wind to the cold North Wind. If they really feel they have been wounded, you may even get the force of a whirlwind. When that happens, watch out, or you might be blown right over.

Butterfly clan people must learn to harness the energy coming through them so that they can ride on it to get to the places they must go in life. If they allow this energy to blow through them without any control they will seem, at best, to be very undirected people, who tend to blow a lot of hot air. At worst, the winds will blow them apart. While air is always present and very necessary for all life to continue, it has a violent as well as a pacific aspect. Butterfly clan people who do not harness their energy properly will be prone to the maladies that take the air out of you, or rip you apart: lung problems, heart problems, strokes and states of mental dissociation. If these problems occur, Butterfly clan people must learn to direct their energy slowly, carefully evaluating which of their many plans are really necessary to their lives.

As parents, Butterfly clan people sometimes sacrifice too much for their children, since the real responsibility of parenthood gives them an overriding direction for a time. They get so caught in this direction that they tend to forget all of their other plans and dreams. Because they take their responsibility so seriously, they make excellent and loving parents, but they will sometimes come to either resent the children for making them miss too much of their own lives or expect too much devotion from them as repayment for all of the sacrifices that they have made.

Butterfly clan children have to be given direction, or their life

---

energies will send them flying so quickly that they won't be able to decide whether to crawl or walk first, whether to wear the red shoes or the black or one of each. Once they have the stability a sense of direction gives them, they are clever, quick, adaptable—and very often smiling or laughing.

People of the Butterfly clan have their major responsibility to the air. They find their own refreshment from being out in a place where there is good clean air that they can breathe in deeply. They also enjoy being outside when the wind is blowing and the air is in the constant movement that they usually feel within themselves. This makes them feel connected to all of the gifts of life that it gives to all of earth's children. It is their responsibility to be aware of the winds and of the things that they accomplish as they blow. Often, Butterfly clan people will have their best inspirations when they are out walking on a windy day.

Otter, Deer and Raven people are those born under the Butterfly clan. These folks will always find themselves wanting to be in a place where they can breathe some good air. If they live in cities, they will be especially sensitive to the pollution of the air and will yearn for weekends in the country or by the ocean, where the wind is always blowing in fresh air. In their lives they will never like to be cooped up in places where the windows don't open. They'll be the ones to always open them up and let the fresh air in. Those born under other elements will come to Butterfly clan places as they travel around the wheel and, at these times, will experience the transforming, gentle, yet constant motion of those of the Butterfly clan. ·

How the Thunderbird Came to Be

Once there was a big hawk, the biggest hawk that had ever lived on the earth. This hawk was so big that his wings darkened two lodges when he flew over the village. Luckily for the people, this hawk was good and kindly toward all those who were around him.

Besides being big, this hawk was also very powerful. He could sing a special song and all of the hawks from all over the territory would come to counsel with him. He could sing another that would catch any rain clouds that were in the vicinity and bring them in toward him. It was even said that he had a song that would make mice and rabbits jump up into his talons when he circled low over the earth. He was a very powerful hawk.

This hawk was so powerful that the Thunder Beings one time decided to give him a special song that he could sing that would draw them to him. They told him that to sing that song correctly he first had to build a circular lodge large enough for himself and all of the other animals he wanted to invite to hear the song. They told him that he had to make a circular altar of a special kind and put particular things from the mineral, the plant and the animal kingdoms on it. They told him that he had to give thanks to the Great Spirit before he sang this song and that he had to feel gratitude to the Thunderers for sharing their power with him.

One summer he decided to sing this song, so he did as the Thunderers had told him. He invited some hawks, an eagle, two ravens, a vulture and an osprey to come into the lodge with him. They accepted, and when the song was done and the Thunderers had come, they all left the lodge knowing that they had been given special power from having heard the song.

Big Hawk had gathered remarkable powers to him, and now a touch of his wings could heal his friends from even the gravest wounds. All of the power that he had became too much for Big Hawk, and, instead of remembering to give thanks every morning to the Great Spirit, he began to get huffed up and to go around singing, "I am the most powerful hawk of them all. I am great Kaik Kaik Kaik."

The Great Spirit looked at the hawk and was patient, hoping that he would remember. But he did not. He just got more and more huffed up.

The next summer he decided that, once again, he would sing

the song of the Thunder Beings so he could get even more power. He decided that he was so powerful he didn't have to bother building the lodge or making the preparations he had been told to make. He didn't even bother to give thanks to the Great Spirit or to the Thunderers. This time he invited all the birds and animals who would come to witness his power.

He began to sing his song just sitting in his nest in the biggest tree around, and he preened himself and huffed himself up more as the Thunderers approached. Suddenly, a bolt of lightning shot out from one of the clouds and burst into a ball of flame just as it touched the tip of Big Hawk's wing. Just as suddenly, the ball of flame and the hawk disappeared before any of the other animals were hurt. All those who had been there looked around, not believing their eyes.

Big Hawk found himself up in the sky talking with the Great Spirit.

"Big Hawk," said the Great Spirit, "you have become too arrogant. You forget to give your thanks. You forget the ceremonies that you have been given. You forget the real source of your power. Since you have insulted the Thunder Beings by misusing the gift that they gave to you, you will now become their servant. You will still be a big handsome bird, but you'll no longer be able to call the thunder. Now they will call you. Whenever the Thunderers go out to do their work, you will go with them. So you don't get too huffed up from people seeing you, you will always be hidden partly behind the clouds. You'll appear to some as a strange cloud formation. You'll appear to others as a fiery shape created by the lightning. Only those with very clear sight will see you as you are, as the bird of fire, the Thunderbird. Go now, and serve those you have hurt until you learn the pleasure that can come from serving and from remembering your place in the universe."

And so the Thunderbird came to the people.

Thunderbird Clan • Fire

Those who are associated by birth with the Thunderbird clan are always actively glowing with the radiant energy of the sun. Like the fire and the sun, they have the capacity to purify themselves and those they touch by reducing matter or spirit to its basic components and then rebuilding with what proves to be real. Their energy is constantly burning within them and usually shining through to those around them. They have the power to bring change, but this change comes from contact with the power that is at their core. They must for a time bring things within their light in order to change them.

Thunderbird people are doers, looking for new things in which to be active. They always seem to be involved in beginning new projects, in burning through the slash around them to make new trails for others to follow. They are often the leaders, in action, in thought and in feeling. They are usually center stage, expressing all of the feelings that burn within them.

Thunderbird people keep turning to their inner fire to find the proper path for them to take. They have strong intuitive energy, and they know enough to use it for guidance. Frequently, they are unable to explain why they think or feel as they do because intuition is not easily put into rational frameworks. They know with an inner knowing why they are doing something, but they are hard put to explain their actions to others, especially to their more logical, cool and calculating companions. Even intellectual Thunderbird clan folks turn to their core for the important decisions of life.

Whenever a new idea or project is getting under way, you will find a person of the Thunderbird clan lending their energy to it. And, while this new idea still interests them, they will make remarkable progress with it. If, however, they have pushed themselves into it too intently, their interest may burn itself out before the project is even near to completion.

Thunderbird clan people are often the brilliant stars in any field who push themselves into prominence with a clever flash of intuition that opens up new pathways. They must be careful not to flash too quickly or they will dim just as fast and find themselves sinking or riding along a trail where their intuition doesn't help them.

Thunderbird clan people tend to be charming and witty, so they make friends quickly. Thunderbird people are clear-sighted. They can see through people more easily than most folks of the other elemental clans. And, being as direct as the sun, what they see they want to say. Whenever they see unnecessary negativity or suffering in others, they want to burn it away so these others can be the pure lights that Thunderbird people see within everyone. Often they will say what they see and then regret their action when the other person seems to not understand what they are trying to do. Thunderbird people are not malicious in their criticisms. Rather, they are sincerely trying to help you to be the great person they feel you can be.

Since their energy can bring about spiritual cleansing, in themselves as well as in others, and since they do have great intuition, Thunderbird people often find themselves in positions of either worldly or spiritual power. When they have attained these positions, they are in for their own most serious testing. Like Big Hawk in the story of this clan, Thunderbird people will sometimes forget where their power is coming from. When that happens they, like the hawk, are in for the purifying flash of lightning fire that makes them less visible to others, reduced to their basic components and ever after mindful of what the source of power really is.

As parents, Thunderbird people sometimes have a lot of problems. Because they are so quick themselves, they find it difficult to adjust themselves to the slow pace of an infant or toddler. They are not the most patient people by nature, and patience is one quality absolutely necessary to be a good parent. Sometimes the experience of parenthood will develop patience in a Thunderbird person and keep them from problems later on. Thunderbird people are generous and loving and will not deny their children anything they want. They tend to be inconsistent disciplinarians, depending on how brightly their own energy is shining at any time, and this can sometimes be confusing to their child. They must learn that children need constant love, patience and attention, and they need to learn how to give this to them at all times, not just when they feel like doing it. They also need to be careful not to dazzle their children so much with their brilliance that the children never want to leave the light of the parents and find the energy within themselves.

Thunderbird children are bright and almost always burning with energy. They have a real inclination to try to learn to do everything they can before they are even out of diapers. These are the precocious children who seem able to do anything— except sit still. They are open, friendly children usually with a ready smile and a big wink.

Like the sun, Thunderbird people are direct and warm and always penetrating. They bring new life to the things that they touch. They open new paths, coax forth new seeds, and heat all around them. If they don't learn to control their heat and their penetration, they will tend to burn themselves out while they are still young. When they are too intense, they will often consume themselves in their own fire. When this happens, they are prone to illnesses that force them to slow down and cool off: heart, head or circulatory problems. To cure themselves, they must learn to temper their light so it shines peacefully as well as actively.

Thunderbird clan people need to be around the sun to feel happy, and to renew themselves. The warmth of the sun soothes them and penetrates to the places where they are tight from their own intensity, causing them to relax. Folks of this clan are also attracted to fire, the sun's gift to the children of the earth. They feel contentment watching the flames of a fire in their fireplace or a campfire. Often they will get their best ideas when they are gazing into flames.

People of this clan are attracted to the lightning that comes with thunderstorms, as this is one of the wildest and most free manifestations of the energy that they always feel within themselves. They like the air better before and after such storms. They seem to take the radiant energy of the lightning within themselves and store it within their own core of light.

Thunderbird clan people have a responsibility to all of these aspects of their element—the sun, fire and lightning. They need to be thankful always for the light and warmth of the sun. They need to be grateful for the Father Sun's gift of fire to warm us when he goes south. They need to understand the power and purpose of the lightning and then give thanks for it.

Red Hawk, Sturgeon and Elk people are those born under the Thunderbird clan. These folks will always want to place themselves in an area where they get good sun at least part of the time and where the thunder and lightning sometimes comes to call to them. They seem to need the energy of natural fire in all of its many forms to strengthen and renew the fire that always burns within them. People born under different elemental signs will come, during their journey around the wheel, to the places of the Thunderbird clan. When they stand in these places, they will experience the radiant energy that comes to those of this clan, and they will experience the cleansing and the energy that this force will give to them.

Frog-Turtle (Water-Earth)

By considering the relationship of the earth to the water, and the water to the earth, it is easy to see how those of the Turtle and Frog clans complement each other. Without the stable base that the earth gives to it, there would be no place for the waters to flow. Without the flowing action of the water, the earth would never change its appearance or its patterns of energy, and would, after a time, dry, crumble and blow away.

So it is with those of the Frog and Turtle clans. Those of the Turtle clan, with their solid, stable energy, build a good foundation, sometimes too good. Along comes a member of the Frog clan with their constantly flowing energy and they find a little crack in the foundation through which they can flow, causing the foundation to shift and change and, eventually, grow to a new form. Without the action of the water steadily washing over it, the earth might never change shape or shift positions. She would become too solid, too unchanging.

Where would those of the Frog clan be without the foundations built by Turtle clan people? Their energy would just be flowing all over the place, without any channels to contain it. They would lack direction and, therefore, would not have the power that direction gives to any person or project. They would be prisoners of the feelings that well up so easily in them, never being able to control them or channel them. What would the Turtle clan people do without those of the Frog clan? They would put their roots down so solidly that they would never budge. They'd become prisoners of their own stability and firm foundations.

People of these two elemental clans provide a balance for each other, as do the actual elements of earth and water. While it is conceivable that the element of earth could exist without the water, what a dry and arid landscape that would be! While you might conceive of a ball of water splashing somewhere in space, what a formless idea that is! Together, the earth and the water create a pleasant picture in one's mind: oceans lapping against the shore, mighty rivers cutting through the mountains, gentle streams running through the forests, lakes silently reflecting the trees around them.

Turtle and Frog clan people make for pleasant combinations that prove fruitful for them and for the people around them. While there will be times of disagreement when water hits a particularly stony spot, or when earth tries to channel rushing water, relationships between people of these clans will cause growth to all of the people involved.

Since Frog clan people empathize so well with others, they will understand the sense of loyalty Turtle clan people need to feel before they enter into a relationship. They'll know how necessary it is for them to keep their word. They'll be able to reflect both the growing and the unchanging parts of the Turtle person's nature, and thus force their friend to be sure they are changing as much as they wish to and in the right areas. They will help to clean out any blockages that are keeping the Turtle clan person's energy from flowing well. They can spark the flow of emotions and help to keep it moving.

In turn, the Turtle clan person can keep his Frog clan friend from flowing and feeling so much that he never gets anything done. With their intelligence, tenacity and craftiness, they can help their Frog clan friends turn their creative, new ideas into something real, with a solid foundation. They can sustain these new ideas during the time when their Frog friend is trying to swim to new waters. Their stiff attitudes are just the thing to knock a hole in the Frog clan person's emotional dam when they are in periods of blocking their energy from flowing.

Emotionally, relationships between people of these clans can work well as the empathetic nature of Frog clan people allows those of the Turtle to be secure enough to open. Conversely, the stability of Turtle folks gives Frog clan people the security to explore the dammed-up parts of their own emotional natures. People of both of these clans aren't too direct and don't push hard, so they allow the other person to open and explore their feelings at their own speed. This is essential because people of both clans consider a direct confrontation as an attack, and they close accordingly.

As people pass through their Frog and Turtle clan positions during their journey around the wheel, they will find that they, too, will benefit from relationships entered into with folks of the complementary clan. These relationships will also benefit the water and the earth as Frog and Turtle clan people learn to combine their energies well in thanks to the elements that help to mold them.

Thunderbird-Butterfly (Fire-Air)

By looking at the relationship of the fire to the air, and the air to the fire, it is obvious why those of the Butterfly and Thunderbird clans complement each other. Without air, fire cannot burn. Without fire and the sun, air would be cold.

It is the same with those of the Butterfly and Thunderbird clans. Those of the Butterfly clan are always moving and trans- forming. They are constantly going from one project to another. When they meet up with one of the Thunderbird clan, with their glowing core and ability to make an idea become a reality, they are carried along by their energy and are able to see one of their thoughts through to completion. Thunderbird clan people, with their active core, would sometimes get stuck too long in one way of being and thinking without the gentle motion that the Butterfly clan members can bring to them.

A fire will glow when the wind is calm, but it bursts into flame when the wind begins to blow. So it is with Thunderbird people. They will harbor an idea or project, putting the solid energy of themselves into its foundation, but never quite get it off the ground until one of the Butterfly clan joins their energy with them.

Butterfly clan people tend to sometimes blow a lot of hot air about all of the things that they could do until a Thunderbird person comes along and burns away all of their mistaken notions of where their energy should go. Butterfly clan people will sometimes appear at the surface, to be cold, because of the airy motion always around them. They need the warmth of the Thunderbird person to make sure that their motion brings growth, not frostbite.

Butterfly clan members can teach their Thunderbird friends of the real pleasure they get from serving others, a lesson that helps to balance the egotistical part of the Thunderbird nature.

They can help to expand the horizons of their Thunderbird clan friends, encouraging them to remove any unnecessary limitations they have placed on themselves. They will quickly see the weak points of any plans their friends are beginning and keep them from making false starts. They can breathe some fresh air into their friends if they are approaching a time of burning out and thus revive them.

Thunderbird clan folks can teach those of the Butterfly clan the power of penetrating any ideas or projects, rather than blowing over their surface. They can help their friends to learn the benefits of going at things directly, rather than in a manipulative way. With their intuition, they can find which new ideas and plans Butterfly folks would be happiest pursuing. When necessary they can bring their burning energy into play to rid their friend of any unnecessary hot air.

Emotionally, Butterfly clan people tend to grow warm, affectionate and friendly once they get to know you and when their energy is flowing well. They seem, however, to be most comfortable with the emotions that are on the surface of their beings. Thunderbird people, on the other hand, tend to feel most things deeply, down in their very core. While they often won't show emotions on the surface, they do feel them very strongly. Together, Butterfly and Thunderbird clan people tend to balance out both of their emotional lives. Butterfly clan people learn to feel things more deeply, and Thunderbird people learn to express some of the things that they feel.

Relationships between people of these two clans will often be tempestuous. They are both active, and they both have the tendency to feel that they are right a good part of the time. However, these relationships are very valuable, as they are ones that cause rapid growth in the people involved and in those around them. Since both clans are active, the people in them have a real liking and respect for each other even if they are in the middle of a violent disagreement. When folks involved in them have gone through their periods of adjustments, relationships between these two clans will be enduring, enjoyable and very productive. As people of other clans step into the positions of those of the Butterfly and Thunderbird clans, they will benefit at those times from the lessons these two complementary clans can help each other to learn.

Butterfly-Turtle (Air-Earth)

Those of the Butterfly and Turtle clans are opposites in many ways. Butterfly people are always in motion, while Turtle people have the stability of the earth. This can be a useful combination if the people in it realize the differences that they have to overcome.

While Frog clan people can wear away the hard spots of Turtle people by their constantly flowing action, Butterfly people cannot. The just don't flow that consistently. When Turtle clan people provide solid earthbound channels for those of the Butterfly clan, they frequently prefer taking off to being brought down to earth.

As the winds change the earth, Butterfly clan people can help Turtle people to grow if they remain warm and teasingly blow away one solid spot and then another. As the earth catches the wind in caves, Turtle clan people can help to direct Butterfly people if they open themselves to them and allow them to come and go as they please. For relationships between these clans to be productive, the people involved need to learn to be loose and playful with each other. When Butterfly clan people send a gust of hot air out, the Turtle person must learn not to turn away, bored or disgusted. When Turtle people forcibly try to give Butterfly people a sense of stability, direction or purpose, they must listen and not just flit off. Relationships between these clans require gentleness and a sense of humor even to begin.

If they can get started in a good way, they can be beneficial to the people involved, as they will learn a great deal from each other. Those of the Butterfly clan will learn to have some stability, direction and loyalty. They'll discover the effect of active energy upon them, and they will sometimes be amazed at the transformation that takes place.

Since they both enjoy serving others, their combined energies will add greatly to any organization with which they are involved by sustaining it while allowing it to change. Because people of both these clans are intelligent, they will usually respect each other's viewpoint, even when they are disagreeing about how quickly new ideas should become a reality. Relationships between people of these clans will also benefit the earth. Without the air and the winds, the seeds on the earth would not be able to pollinate, spread and grow. Without the earth, the winds would be merely howling energy, with nothing to direct them or give them a purpose for being.

Butterfly-Frog (Air-Water)

Those of the Butterfly and Frog clans have the similarities that their flowing natures give to them. They both always seem to be moving physically, mentally and emotionally. While those of the Butterfly clan move quickly, often flying from one thought or project to another, those of the Frog clan usually move steadily. Their movement is a bit more reliable than that of Butterfly clan people.

Because of their similarities, Butterfly and Frog clan people will often find fault with each other. They see their own weaknesses magnified and reflected by those of the other clan. Together they will tend not to have much direction, since they both are always in motion, albeit motions of a different kind.

If they are able to persevere through their original period of reflection, people of these clans will find that they are able to be of great comfort to each other. Since they have similar natures, they are able to understand each other and encourage each other to grow in all of the ways that they can. However, for relationships between these clans to endure, one of the people involved will have had to move around the wheel enough to understand the stability of the Turtle and Thunderbird clans so that they are able to bring some direction to the relationship. Without this, both people will tend to keep moving without any goals, and they will find it difficult to complete anything that they have begun, or even to decide what projects they should work on together.

From their Frog clan friends, Butterfly people can learn to bring change in a more predictable, steadily flowing manner. They can learn to take time to feel things more deeply, to empathize more with those they know. They can begin to clear out some of the blockages that their tendency to express only surface emotions may have created. From Butterfly clan folks, those of the Frog clan can learn to use their deep feelings to transform themselves and things around them. They may come to see weak points in some plans they have long held on to and thus free any energy they have been holding back.

Since people of both clans are creative and like new plans and ideas, when they work together on a chosen goal they can bring a lot of fresh, good energy to it.

With some channeling of both people's energies, relationships between these clans can be healing, transforming and creative. It is the air that causes water to move, rather than stagnate. It is the water that brings moisture to the air so that rain can come to the earth. When people of these clans are together and have learned how to work well, their joint energy can help to bring healing to the earth and to all of her children.

Thunderbird-Frog (Fire-Water)

Those of the Thunderbird and Frog clans have much that they can teach each other. While they are opposites, they both can help to bring major changes in the other. Water turns fire from a blazing flame to a small cinder and eventually puts it out. Fire causes water to heat, boil and evaporate. When members of these elemental clans get together, they can change each other as much as their elements can if they know when to stop. If they don't, they can seriously hurt each other.

Frog people can often frustrate those of the Thunderbird, because of their quicksilver nature. When a fire person begins to know people of the water clan, he will want to bring some of his radiant glow to their sometimes too fluid natures. He will attempt directly to tell the other how to improve and strengthen. In turn, the water person will attempt to seep past what he sees as a direct attack and will often try to dampen some of the flames he feels enfolding him. If people of these clans can get past this point undamaged, they have a chance to build a relationship that can be helpful to them both.

From Thunderbird people, the Frog clan members can learn a little of pulsating, radiant energy which can warm them to the core of their beings. They can find new ways to direct themselves and to channel the moving energy always going through them. They will find how to see things more clearly and with more optimism. From Frog clan members, the Thunderbird people can learn how to temper their flames, how to let their energies become calm while still radiant. They can learn how to empathize more with others and let out some of their own deep feelings. They'll learn how to let the beginnings they choose be guided by the universal flow of energies, rather than by their own wills. They can learn how to control their fire so it helps, rather than destroys.

In their sun aspects Thunderbird people can help to warm the sometimes cool nature of the Frog people, as the sun warms a pond or a lake. In this warming, there will be some evaporation that will change the nature of the water, but it will be gentle change. The Thunderbird people, like the sun, have the power of penetration of water, as well as earth and air. This penetration changes the natures of the other elements, but in a gradual and loving manner. By watching how the water accepts the changes their penetration causes, the Thunderbird people can learn some of the lessons of patience and acceptance that are necessary to temper their natures.

When people of these clans learn to join their energies, they can help to bring the rain of emotions that will enable the earth and all of her children to grow.

Thunderbird-Turtle (Fire-Earth)

People of the Thunderbird and Turtle clans have many things that are common to both of their natures. While those of the Thunderbird clan tend to be more active in their way of living, people of both clans have the stability that a solid core gives to them. Because of these similarities they, like those of the Butterfly and Frog clans, will often mirror traits to each other that are difficult to accept and deal with. This can cause disruptiveness in the beginning of any relationship between people of these clans. If they can weather this initial discomfort, the relationship can be a very growing one for both people involved.

At the core of the earth is the fire, the light of the earth which is similar in nature to the light of the sun. Without this core of light, the earth would not be a living being. Without the light of the Father Sun, all of earth's children would cease growing. Without the earth to shine upon, the sun would not be fulfilling all of his mission. Without the earth, fire would run out of materials on which it could burn. The sun and the earth need each other to be able to accomplish their purposes in being.

It is the same for people of these two clans. Turtle people in their solid stability need the warmth of the sun to allow them to move, rather than freeze. Thunderbird people need the solid foundation of Turtle people for their fire to burn bright enough. While they are both stable in their natures, the earth is more stable than the fire.

From their Thunderbird friends Turtle people can learn to have less fear of change, to have more clarity of vision, to make quicker beginnings. They can become warmer, more penetrating and more optimistic. In turn, Thunderbird clan members can learn the benefits of keeping their word and of staying with a project even though it is already under way. They can learn how to sustain as well as start something, and the pleasure of serving as well as leading.

Relationships between people of these clans tend to grow steadily after any initial disagreement. They can be the most solid of any elemental relationships if they are nurtured well as they grow. Through this association Turtle people will discover the core of energy that is the base of their beings, and Thunderbird people will learn how to put ever firmer foundations under anything that they do.

Same Clan Combinations

People who share the same elemental clan will share the basic nature that their element gives to them. Because of this, they will find it easy to understand each other. They will share some likes and dislikes, strengths and weaknesses. They'll tend to come in contact frequently, as they like to be in the same sorts of places. They will find easy agreement on most superficial matters.

However, their similarities can make deeper relationships difficult. As people of the same clan open to each other, they see their own strengths and weaknesses in someone else. It is never pleasant to see a trait you don't like in yourself magnified in someone else. If you haven't accepted that trait and learned to deal with it, nothing will bother you more. If you are unwilling to deal with your own weaknesses, you'll get to really dislike being around someone who reminds you of them. When you reach this point with someone else who shares your elemental clan, you'll have to decide whether to begin working on yourself or whether to walk away from the relationship.

Because of this mirroring effect, same clan relationships are often difficult ones if the people involved wish to be really close to each other. If the people involved are open to working on themselves, these relationships can be really valuable tools. If they don't wish to change, it is usually necessary for them to back off from the person involved. However, same clan relationships make very pleasant associations if they are on a lighter level. People of the same clan will find it easy to agree on what to do and where to go.

In nature, like attracts like. Things of the earth return to their source. Rain clouds are attracted to bodies of water. Winds blow in areas where other winds have already been. Fire joins with other fire to make larger flames. Like the elements, people of the same clan can do much good for the earth and their relations on her if they can join together and work in a good manner. To do so on a deep level, they must be willing, first, to do any work that they need to upon themselves.

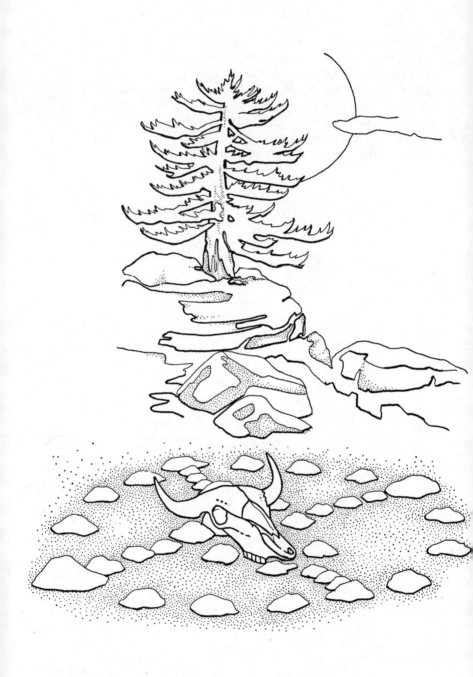

TRAVELING
THE MEDICINE WHEEL

The Medicine Wheel is divided into twelve moons, or months, beginning with the Earth Renewal Moon, which comes on December 22. You begin your journey at one of these moons. Your starting position gives you the strengths, lessons and challenges of one set of totems. It also gives you your beginning elemental clan and your beginning Spirit Keeper.

By learning from these, you expand yourself to know some of your relations on the Earth Mother. You can learn about your moon, totems, clan and Spirit Keeper by observing and reading about the minerals, plants, animals, elements and winds that share this association. You are unique so you will share some characteristics of all of these, but you won't share all of them.

As you travel through your life, you may observe that your beginning totems no longer seem to fit you. Perhaps you came in as a Cougar, but you no longer feel a connection with this animal. When you see a red hawk in the sky, it makes your spirit soar. You begin to take on the leadership of some projects with which you are involved. You notice that you are more direct in your speaking, that you feel less wary of people in general. This means that you have stepped around the wheel. You no longer stand in the place of the Cougar. You are now a person of the Budding Trees Moon, with the red hawk as your animal totem. You have taken one step around the Medicine Wheel, and you have a whole new set of helpers and of lessons.

Because the Medicine Wheel is based upon the solar cycle, people commonly travel in a sunwise direction. However, that is not the only way that they can travel. A person who began at the Frogs Return Moon might find that the next position they occupy is that of the Harvest Moon, with the totems of the Brown Bear, the violet and the amethyst. This means that they are traveling the wheel by going from one moon of the Turtle elemental clan to another. They could expect that they would next come to the place of the Snow Goose people.

Others might travel the wheel by going from one position to the complementary position, as Otter people would do if they found themselves in the place of the Sturgeon folks. Others can travel the wheel in a random fashion. No one else can tell you how to travel the wheel, although others may be able to help you understand the positions in which you have been, and those you may be traveling toward.

It does not matter in which direction you travel the wheel as long as you keep traveling. The only way you can stop your own growth is to cling to the strengths of one position and refuse to let go of them. When you do this, you block your own energies, and you make it more difficult for those around you to continue their journey.

If you refuse to leave a position when you have learned its lessons, then you block the travels of someone else who needs to enter your position for his own growth. As each person learns of his place and its powers, he moves forward around the wheel. As we open up, giving and receiving, we expand ourselves until there is nothing in our mind's sight but the Medicine Wheel. It becomes the universe and helps us to search out the distant truths.

When you stand at your beginning totem, you first learn how to make your prayers and you ask to learn about the powers of your totems. Once you push aside your ego, you are able to experience the thoughts and feelings of how that particular totem relates to the natural forces. Then your body remains, but your heart and mind are free to take off and you can travel across the land experiencing the world as a snow goose, an otter, a cougar, a red hawk, a beaver, a deer, a flicker, a sturgeon, a brown bear, a raven, a snake, an elk. You share the power of that creature, and then you grow with it.

It is possible for some people to travel the wheel in one lifetime. For others, more time might be necessary. For some, one trip around the wheel is sufficient. For others, more are needed. Life is a circle spiraling upward as well as outward. There are many levels of lessons that each of us needs to learn as we travel through life. We are all unique, and we all must travel the Medicine Wheel in our own way and at our own rate of speed.

When we come to the wheel we pray, "Great Spirit, I come searching for help. I am a poor person. Please guide me. Send me the knowledge of what my course shall be." In this manner people come to seek their power. You can do the same thing.

Find your place on the Medicine Wheel, whether or not it is the same one where you began. Center yourself and then reach out. As your mind releases all things of daily life, you become free. There is nothing else in the world. No place else but where you are. And now you open up. Your mind energy surges out. You ride on the wind to the most distant places. You are free to search. You can feel and blend your energy with the natural forces. All of life becomes a song. You are part of the song of life. You become one with a hawk, an eagle, a bear, a rock. You are now a hawk dreaming of a person. Wherever your spirit will take you, you follow it. You are free to seek out the outermost or innermost parts of the universe.

In order to grow you must reach out and give of yourself to the universe. You give and you grow in experiencing the universe. No teacher can teach a selfish person. If you have a mind lock that locks you into one position, you will not grow beyond that. To receive knowledge, you must first give, because the giving process opens you up. In the process of life you breathe in air, and then expel it. The plants use this air that you expel to breathe and reprocess. Similarly, when you make love, it is a giving and receiving process. One cannot live unto oneself. Accept that and you accept one of the great laws of the universe. Traditional Native people accepted that law, and they kept in balance with everything around them. That is why they were able to live for thousands of years on this land, and yet, when early explorers came here, they spoke of it as a great unspoiled wilderness. The teaching of the Medicine Wheel is balance and harmony. Once you have opened yourself up to giving and accepting, you may start around the wheel.

In times past, our Native people had a very strong contact with the natural forces. When we would make prayers for rain, the rain would come. When we were hungry, we held a buffalo dance and sang to the buffalo, and they heard our songs and came. It's possible to reestablish that relationship, but people must stop and put aside their haughty ways and learn to seek harmony with the rest of the Creation. They must seek to blend with nature, rather than to conquer her. When a person is a true seeker, the universe will open up to him or her. When you come to the Medicine Wheel and take your place in a good manner, all things come to you.

CONSTRUCTING
A MEDICINE WHEEL

The Medicine Wheel, in all of its forms, has the power and the ability to connect you to infinity. After reading of this vision, you may feel it is right for you to construct a Medicine Wheel of your own. In our vision of the wheel, we saw many such newly built wheels spread across the land, and we saw people learning to use them in a proper manner that will help with their healing and evolution and with the healing of the Earth Mother.

Before telling you how to construct a wheel, we would like to give you some basic information about some of the ceremonies that can be connected with such construction. What we are sharing here are the ceremonies that we use in connection with our own life and Medicine Wheel. These are based upon the Native way, but come also from our own visions. These can provide a guideline for you in the time when you are becoming familiar with your Medicine Wheel. However, you should, when it feels right, use your own vision and intuition to guide you in developing the ceremonies that are right for you and for your Medicine Wheel. We all have our own prayer, placed in our hearts at the time of our birth, and our own songs, and these are the prayers we should make and the songs we should sing. We can share with you the way in which we pray, but your real prayer must come from within your heart.

Before beginning any of our other ceremonies, we smudge the people who are going to be present. Smudging is a process of using smoke to clear away any negative energies and to attract positive energies to you. We use a large shell as the container for the sage and sweet grass that we burn. You might also wish to use a pottery or stone bowl. If you can't locate sage or sweet grass, you might wish to smudge with tobacco. Use a good grade of tobacco with as few additives as possible. You light the herb with either a coal or a match and blow out the flames so it is smoldering, rather than burning. To keep it smoldering you may fan it with your hand, a feather or a fan.

The person who is doing the smudging first brings the smoke toward his or her heart and then up over his head. This will help his energy to run in a good direction, and it will take any negative thoughts or feelings out of him. He then offers the bowl to the four directions, the Father Sun and the Earth Mother. He takes the bowl around to the people participating. They should be standing in a circle, and the bowl should be taken in a sunwise direction, beginning with the North.

Following the smudging of the people present, we smudge our pipe and tobacco and have a pipe ceremony. To Native people, the pipe represents the universe. In it, all of the kingdoms are brought together. The bowl is made of stone to represent the mineral kingdom. The stem is wood, representing the plant kingdom. It is decorated with fur and feathers, representing the animal kingdom, and it is used by a person, representing the human kingdom. When we put the tobacco into the bowl, we offer a pinch for each of these kingdoms, for the four elements, for the spirit kingdoms, for the Earth Mother, the Father Sun, the Grandmother Moon and the Great Spirit. When we light the pipe, we offer a puff of smoke to each of the directions, to the earth and to the Great Spirit. With the smoke, an ethereal substance capable of penetrating between the realms of the physical and spiritual worlds, go our prayers. These prayers are not just for humans, but for all of those we have remembered in preparing the pipe. They are prayers for unity, for healing and for proper direction.

After the pipe ceremony, we attend to whatever other needs have brought us together. Sometimes we meet at the Medicine Wheel to have healing circles for people who have asked for our help with their healing, and for the Earth Mother. Sometimes we meet to perform and witness a marriage of two people, or to welcome a little one who is beginning his or her travels on the earth. We meet there to send people out on their vision quests and to welcome new members into our medicine society. We meet there to celebrate the turning of the seasons. Our Medicine Wheel has become the focal point for the ceremonial life of our community.

In our ceremonies, we do ask menstruating sisters to stand away from the Medicine Wheel, because the strong power coming through them at this time could affect the other powers that we are using in the ceremonies. We do this with the full agreement of the sisters, since they have come to recognize the strength of their own female powers and the years of training it takes to be able to channel them.

Preceding some of our ceremonies we, and the people participating with us, fast for a period of time ranging from twenty-four hours to four days. Following some ceremonies we have ceremonial meals in which we remember all the gifts of food our relations give to us. Following all ceremonies we have a good feed.

At some points during the year we will have giveaways. These are times when we give gifts to those present so they can share the happiness that we are feeling and so they will have something by which to remember the moment of shared happiness. The gifts do not have to be elaborate, but they should be gifts from the heart. In the old times, giveaways followed marriages, births, deaths, puberty ceremonies and times of good—or bad—fortune.

Whatever ceremony we are observing at our Medicine Wheel, we ask all people present to share what is in their hearts. To do this we sometimes pass a talking stick around the circle, in a sunwise direction. We have a beaded stick, but you could use a branch from a tree. As the stick is passed around, people may say what they feel or they may pass it on. At other times we pass around a bag of cornmeal or tobacco and ask each person to take a pinch and offer it to the Earth Mother. As they make their offering, they may make a prayer silently or out loud. During some ceremonies we pass around a bowl of water and ask people to share a drink with us, remembering the good gift of water that we have been given.

To construct a Medicine Wheel you will need thirty-five rocks, and a special rock, or horns or antlers, for the center. Alternatively, you can choose to make a sacred fire pit as the center of your wheel. You can build your wheel alone or with others. It is a good way of beginning to share a special energy with people that you know.

You should carefully select the site for your Medicine Wheel. It should be an area that makes you feel good, strong, powerful and open to all of your relations. It needs to have a fairly flat area four to eight feet in diameter. Once your wheel is built, you will want people to respect it by not casually walking into it or across it, so you should pick an area that does not have a lot of traffic. If you can't find a spot without traffic, just pick one that makes you feel right and smudge the wheel itself each time before you use it.

Choose rocks that feel right to you. It is good to take the people who will help construct the Medicine Wheel with you when you select stones. Remember to leave an offering of cornmeal or tobacco for the rocks that you take. After getting the rocks, leave them in an area a little away from where the diameter of the Medicine Wheel will be.

It is good to construct your wheel early in the morning. The first rays of the sun give a special energy. You may begin with smudging and then have a pipe ceremony if anyone feels good about conducting that. Let people express their feelings, then take some silent time to center yourselves. The person organizing the construction should announce that the construction is to begin with the center, the Creator's eye, the place of compacting power. Then he or she should either dig the fire pit or put the stone or horns in place.

The organizer should then ask for people who feel a special connection to each of the elemental clans, the Father Sun, the Grandmother Moon and the Earth Mother, to each select a stone and place it around the center object in a circle one to two feet in diameter. Next, people who feel a good connection to each of the four Spirit Keepers should select a stone and place it in the correct position. These rocks should be at the four directional points of the outside diameter of the circle.

If there is a person present who began his or her life at each of the twelve moons of the Medicine Wheel, he or she should take a stone and place it in the correct position. If there isn't, people who feel a good connection with the moon and its totems should do so. Finally, you should place the pathways between the four quarters of the universe. These are spokes that radiate out from the inside circle of seven rocks to the rock representing each Spirit Keeper. When constructing these, remember that they are the paths used by the Spirit Keepers as they go about their work to help with the healing and evolution of the planet.

When you have finished constructing the wheel, give people an opportunity to speak what is in their hearts, whether it be words, a poem, a prayer or music.

If you have chosen to place a fire pit at the center of the circle, you should remember that this will only be used for sacred, ceremonial fires. These are usually begun before sunrise by a person chosen to be the fire keeper. Begin them in the most natural way possible, using pine needles and cones, or grass, for kindling, and using a flint or matches, not a lighter or any kind of starting fluid. Never allow anyone to throw anything into the fire. Use wood that has been gathered with proper thanksgiving. When you see the smoke circling in all four directions, you know that the fire has been properly prepared. Be very aware of the surrounding earth conditions when you build such a fire so that you do not endanger any of your relations. When the ceremony is completed, the fire keeper should dismantle any wood remaining in the fire and then put out the coals with water or earth.

Once your wheel is constructed, you should use it frequently. It is a good place to go to refresh your energy or to build your strength. Try standing in the different positions on the wheel and see how each one affects the level of your energy. Learn of the powers of the directions, of the powers of the elements, of the lessons of the moon. Each position can give you new growth, new understanding. If you feel good about a direction, an element or a moon, go to your Medicine Wheel then, too, and give your thanks for the good thing that you have learned or discovered.

If you find that you are having trouble feeling the different energies of the Medicine Wheel, here are some thoughts to help you. Before you come to the circle, place your hands on the Earth Mother. Try to feel the natural life force surging within. Embrace a tree until you can feel the life force within it. A tree is like a pipeline or conductor bringing energy from the sky to the earth. The same life force energy surges through all life. When you embrace someone and you feel good energy surging between you, that is the same life force energy that is in the trees and the other creatures. Only now we have been taught to experience it more strongly between two people.

It is the blending of the male and female energy that brings forth new life. This same force can give you the power to heal someone. Learn these things. Let the Medicine Wheel help you to open up to the universe.

Sun Bear is a Chippewa medicine man who has founded The Bear Tribe, located near Spokane, Washington, which welcomes Indians and non-Indians as members. The editor of the magazine *Many Smokes,* he is also a lecturer, teacher and author of two previous books, *At Home in the Wilderness* and *Buffalo Hearts.* Wabun, his wife (born Marlise Ann James), holds an M.S. from the Columbia School of Journalism, has written articles for magazines such as *Life, McCall's,* and *New York,* and is author of the book *The People's Lawyers.*

If you would like to write to Sun Bear and Wabun, their address is:

> Sun Bear and Wabun
> ℅ The Bear Tribe
> P.O. Box 9167
> Spokane, Washington 99209

Please enclose a stamped, self-addressed envelope if you wish to have a reply.